Looking at
BUTTERFLIES

Looking at
BUTTERFLIES

L. Hugh Newman

Edited by
George E. Hyde

Illustrated by
Anthony Moore

COLLINS
St James's Place London

William Collins Sons & Co Ltd
London · Glasgow · Sydney · Auckland
Toronto · Johannesburg

First published 1959
This edition published 1977

© L. Hugh Newman, 1977

ISBN 0 00 219688 3

Made and Printed in Great Britain by
William Collins Sons & Co Ltd Glasgow

FOREWORD

Since the publication in 1959 of the first edition of this book there have been considerable changes in the butterfly population of Britain. Because a few brightly coloured species such as the Small Tortoiseshell, the Peacock and the Red Admiral are often seen in gardens, casual observers are apt to believe that all is well with butterflies generally, but unfortunately this is not so. Amongst the several causes of decline are the destruction of haunts and increased urbanization, and these are likely to increase in the future. Species already in danger of disappearing from our countryside include the Large Blue, Large Tortoiseshell and Chequered Skipper, and there are others which might soon follow. We can only hope that they will manage to survive for future generations to enjoy. Collecting butterflies has long been a popular hobby, but a growing number of people now prefer to photograph the insects alive rather than amassing large numbers of dead specimens. This is all to the good, but it is only fair to add that we owe much of our present knowledge of butterflies to earlier generations of collectors.

For help over the distribution maps (pages 129–44) I am most grateful to the Biological Records Centre at the Monks Wood Experimental Station, Abbots Ripton, Huntingdon; and to Mr N. D. Riley.

CONTENTS

DESCRIPTIONS

CONTENTS

8

PLATES

9

GLOSSARY

Ab.   aberration, different from the normal within a species
Androconia   scent scales on the wings of male butterflies
Antennae   feelers on the butterfly's head, used for touch and smell
Anus   opening at the hind end of the body
Apex   tip of wing
Chequered   square markings on the wings
Chrysalis   (= pupa) stage in development between caterpillar and butter-
   fly, when great internal changes are occurring
Conical   tapering from a circular base to a point
Cuticle   thin protective skin on a leaf
Diffused   not clearly defined, spread out
Discoidal cell   ringed spot in centre of wing
Dorsal   upper surface, back of body
Girdle   silken thong around body of chrysalis
Gregarious   living together in a colony
Gynandrous, gynandromorph   part male and part female
Hibernaculum   the structure made by those caterpillars which hibernate
Hibernation   winter sleep
Hermaphrodite   half male and half female
Homoeosis   assuming the appearance of another part
Imago   the perfect insect, butterfly
Immigrant   insect crossing the sea to breed (where possible) in Britain
Iridescent   multi-coloured, rainbow-like
Larva   caterpillar
Lateral   side, of body
Longitudinal   running lengthwise
Lunules   crescent-shaped marks on wings
Marginal   edge of wing
Melanic   when the dark brown or black pigment is in excess of normal
Nectar   sweet liquid obtained from flowers
Nervures   struts supporting an insect's wing
Oblique   slanting
Ochreous   yellowish shade
Opaque   not transparent
Points   raised spots on body
Pupa   chrysalis
Pupate   turn into chrysalis, third stage in life history
Pupil   centre part of eye

Reticulated   marked with network of fine lines
Scale   minute section of wing
Scalloped   wavy edge
Segment   one division of the body
Spiracles   breathing holes in the sides of insects
Striated   streaked with narrow black lines
Subsp.   (= sub-species) a well established local race, differing from the type
Suffused   spread over in relation to colours
Tawny   yellowish-brown
Translucent   semi-transparent
Tubercles   small swellings or bumps
Ultramarine   sky blue
Var.   variety, different from the type
Variegated   marked differently in various colours
Vein   one of the small branching ribs of a butterfly's wing
Ventral   under-surface of body

THE STRUCTURE OF BUTTERFLIES

In its imago stage, as a fully developed insect, a butterfly has two pairs of wings. These consist of a thin membrane, supported by hollow ribs known as veins. Before the wing is expanded it is something like a deflated bag, the upper and under surfaces being separated, but as it expands the two layers are drawn together by contracting strands and finally join up to form a single membrane. This is transparent, but covered with innumerable small coloured scales, arranged like the tiles on a roof and fitting by their short stalks into minute sockets on the wing. The shape and colour of the scales varies in different butterflies, and it is these scales which give the wings their colour and pattern. Some male butterflies have patches of dark scent scales or androconia on their fore-wings. The scales serve to distribute scent produced by glands on the wing and may become detached during courtship flight. The wings are often edged with a fringe of hair-like scales and similar scales cover the body of the insect.

The head is clearly divided from the thorax, or fore-body, and carries two slender antennae, or feelers, with clubbed tips. These are organs of sense and balance and are in constant play while the insect is active. On either side of the head is a large bulbous compound eye, consisting of innumerable small hexagonal facets, over 6000 in all. The mouth parts of a butterfly are not adapted for chewing or biting, but have been modified into a long tube or proboscis, usually referred to as the tongue. This consists of two halves, joined together by small hooks to form a hollow tube through which the insect can suck up fluids. When not in use the tongue remains coiled up like a watch spring underneath the head.

The thorax bears the wings and the legs. The latter are six in number, one pair on each segment, but in many butterflies the first pair is reduced to mere stumps. The legs are jointed and made up of nine separate parts, ending in two claws. The third pair is furnished with extra-sensory organs, with the aid of which butterflies can distinguish the taste of sweet liquids and recognize the texture of the leaves of their food plants.

The abdomen consists of ten segments and contains the reproductive organs. In male butterflies there is also a pair of well-developed claspers, called anal-claspers, on the ninth segment. They are used for holding the body of the female during pairing. The abdomen is generally larger in the female than the male.

Like all other insects, a butterfly has no internal skeleton, and its body is supported by the tough external skin of a horn-like substance called chitin. The breathing apparatus consists of a series of fine tubes, called trachae, which run all over the body. The air enters into this system through the spiracles, round openings along the sides of the body, two on each segment.

The blood is a more or less colourless fluid, contained in the body cavity, and not in veins. It is kept circulating by the regular contraction of a tube-shaped heart, situated along the back. The central nervous system consists of two separate cords, lying close together on the bottom of the body cavity, and there is a fairly complex, two-part brain in the head. The digestive system is simple, consisting only of the alimentary tract. The food is absorbed in the coiled portion called the mid-gut.

LIFE HISTORY

The Egg

A butterfly undergoes a complete metamorphosis before reaching maturity and passes through three distinct stages; egg, caterpillar and chrysalis, finally emerging as the imago. After mating most female butterflies carefully select the correct food plant on which to lay their eggs. These are laid either singly or in large batches and to the naked eye look like small elongated or round grains. Under the microscope, however, they show an amazing variety and complexity in shape and surface decoration. Most of the primitive Skippers lay smooth-shelled eggs but in all the other butterflies the surface is either decorated with a raised honeycomb or fine ridges or flanges running from the top of the egg to the flattened base. The egg of the White Admiral is covered in spines like a sea urchin.

The length of time spent in the egg stage varies greatly in different butterflies, and may be anything from a week to nine months in the case of those which overwinter as eggs. The eggs often change colour, usually becoming darker with age, and shortly before hatching the tiny caterpillar can be seen through the semi-transparent shell. Many young caterpillars eat the whole, or part of their egg shells. This applies particularly to those which go into hibernation immediately after hatching. In many cases this meal of egg-shell is vital and the caterpillar will die if deprived of it.

The Caterpillar

The caterpillars of the British butterflies vary a good deal in size and shape, some being long and narrow while others are short and humped. Fundamentally, however, they are all similar, their bodies consisting of a head and thirteen segments. The head may be quite large and easily visible, or it may be small and almost hidden under a bulging first segment. On the head are two groups of six small, simple eyes, which most probably can only distinguish between light and darkness. Instead of long antennae there is a pair of very small feelers, invisible to the naked eye. The mouthparts are entirely different to those of a butterfly, consisting of powerful biting jaws, called mandibles. Directly beneath the mouth is a spinneret, a small perforated projection through which the liquid silk produced by the silk glands flows out when required. The first three segments of the body correspond to the segments of the thorax in the imago and each one carries a pair of short jointed legs, ending in claws. The two following segments have no legs, but segments six to ten carry a pair of short, unjointed feet, called prolegs, furnished with sucker pads. On the last segment is a similar, but larger pair of feet called claspers. In the Skipper family the last segment is furnished with a curious structure known as the anal comb. This is mobile and is used by the caterpillar for throwing its excrement out of the shelter in which it hides.

Most caterpillars are solitary, but in those species where the eggs are laid in large batches, the larvae live gregariously, at least during the early stages. With the exception of the Large White, gregarious caterpillars are only found among the Fritillaries and the Vanessas. Butterfly larvae feed on a great variety of plants, and there is a tendency for closely related species to feed on plants belonging to the same botanical group. Some species are restricted to a single food-plant, while others will eat a variety of alternative foods. The manner of feeding is often characteristic of each species and a knowledgeable entomologist can tell with some accuracy, by the way leaves have been nibbled or perforated, which species of caterpillar is responsible. Some species feed only at night, hiding away during daylight hours, while others are active in the daytime, resting at night. Most caterpillars consume a large quantity of food before reaching their full size. A few species are cannibals, especially in the early stages, attacking and eating younger and weaker members of their own kind. In this way the first larva to hatch on a twig will eat any eggs and younger larvae in the vicinity. The great majority of caterpillars, however, are vegetarians throughout their lives, the most notable exception being the Large Blue, which feeds on the larvae of ants, after it has completed its third moult.

During the caterpillar stage the skin is shed several times. The number of skin changes, or instars, varies with the species but is normally four. One exception to this rule is the Large Skipper, which moults six times before reaching maturity. Larvae usually change a good deal in appearance during their period of growth, assuming new colours and gaining or losing hairs and spines. An outstanding example of this is the Swallow-tail, which begins as a black larva and ends up a brilliant green, marked with black and orange. As space does not allow a full description of all stages of the larvae in this book, only the final full-fed caterpillar has been described, with brief indications of other colours when necessary. Many hibernating caterpillars change colour during the winter, becoming more dull and drab and then resuming a green tint in the spring. Although some butterfly caterpillars appear quite smooth to the naked eye, when viewed through a microscope they will be found to have a covering of hairs or bristles, and various raised warts and markings on the skin. It is the habit of many larvae to eat their cast skins.

The colouring of caterpillars varies very much, but usually blends well with their surroundings. Exceptions are those with warning colours, such as the Swallow-tail, the Large White, and the black, spiny larvae of Vanessas and Fritillaries, which are distasteful to birds. Most caterpillars contrive to hide themselves more or less, either by feeding on the lower surface of leaves, or making a shelter by drawing together parts of their food-plant with strands of silk. Some take refuge in webs of silk and others burrow into seed pods or buds so that they are hidden from view.

The caterpillar stage of a butterfly's life may be fairly brief, especially in species which have several successive broods during the summer; in the Green-veined White for example, the caterpillar feeds up in eighteen days. On the other hand it may last over nine months in those species which hibernate as caterpillars. Many butterflies overwinter in the caterpillar stage, some in complete hibernation, others more or less torpid, but waking and feeding on mild days. When ready for pupation the caterpillar very often changes colour, becoming darker, often with a dull pink or purplish tinge, while the body contracts and becomes thicker. It stops feeding and wanders about searching for a suitable place in which to pupate.

The Chrysalis

The majority of butterflies pupate fully exposed, or only protected by very flimsy cocoons of a few silk threads. The Skippers are an exception, making fairly strong cocoons inside folded blades of grass. A small number of butterflies burrow just under the surface of the soil before pupating, or hide away amongst debris on the ground.

Before changing into a chrysalis the caterpillar usually secures itself to some support, either by spinning a pad of silk under its hind-claspers and a girdle of silk round the middle of the body, so that it is held in position close to the surface of the leaf or stem, or else by merely spinning a pad of silk and then hanging suspended from this, head downwards, gripping the pad with the claspers. The final skin change, which reveals the pupa, does not take place for some little while after the caterpillar has prepared itself for pupation. Sometimes two or three days may elapse before the change. Eventually the skin splits along the thorax and by wriggling movements the chrysalis gradually works the skin backwards until it is free. Sometimes the skin remains attached to the chrysalis, in other cases it is completely discarded, or shrivels and drops off. Most butterfly chrysalids are supplied with a number of fine hooks at the tail end, usually springing from an elongated portion known as a cremaster. Sometimes a similar structure exists on the head. These hooks are fixed into the silk pad or the inside of the cocoon and keep the chrysalis securely in place.

The pupa is at first soft and moist, but very soon the surface hardens. It is quite unlike the caterpillar to look at, resembling more closely the perfect insect, and on the surface the various parts of the butterfly can be seen. The wing cases are clearly visible and so are the legs, the tongue and the eyes. The only openings are the spiracles or breathing holes along the sides. The chrysalis stage, or pupal stage, is a resting period when no nourishment is taken, and complicated changes take place inside the shell. The body breaks down almost completely into a fluid and then gradually builds up again into all the organs of the fully developed imago. Many chrysalids are able to move to a limited degree, and wriggle if disturbed, but they cannot crawl away. The Vanessa butterflies and the Fritillaries are especially mobile as pupae, while the chrysalids of Hairstreaks, Blues, Coppers and a few others appear to be unable to make any movement.

Chrysalids are generally rather dull in colour, but some are decorated with gleaming metallic spots, like silver or gold. The ground colour is often variable and matches the object to which the chrysalis is attached. The surface is usually rather rough and there are often numerous sharp points and projections. The length of time spent in the chrysalis stage varies greatly. With summer butterflies that have two or three broods it may be only a fortnight or so, while those which pass the winter as pupae remain in this stage for nine months.

Shortly before the butterfly emerges the wings colour up and can be seen quite clearly through the pupal shell. Most of the colours on the wings of butterflies are pigments; metallic brilliance and blue and purple sheens which vary in different lights are due to diffraction of light from the scales. When emergence takes place the chrysalis splits at the back of the head and the butterfly pulls itself out of the shell. This is not always an easy development, and if it does not take place quickly the insect may become a cripple. As soon as the butterfly is free it climbs upwards to a vantage point where it can hang by its feet while the wings expand.

To begin with the wings are only about one-tenth of the size they will grow to when fully expanded, but as fluid is pumped into them from the body, and the strands connecting the upper and lower surface contract, so the wings spread out. This happens quite rapidly, usually in about half an hour, but for some time afterwards the wings remain soft and damp and the butterfly continues to hang motionless until they have had time to dry and harden. On a warm and sunny day it will be ready for its first flight within an hour of emerging, and unlike a fledgling bird, it does not have to learn to fly, but can flutter easily from flower to flower, or soar up towards the light with perfect skill.

BREEDING BUTTERFLIES

The surest way of getting perfect specimens for a collection is to breed butterflies in captivity whenever possible. Many species are easy to rear, and the collector will learn many interesting details about their life histories by observing them at close quarters during this period. Field work is of course necessary at the same time, in order to obtain the live female, the eggs or the larvae, which are to serve as foundation stock for breeding.

Eggs

Searching for butterfly eggs requires both patience and skill, except for a few species whose eggs are easily seen. Eggs of the Large and Small Whites can be found in gardens on cabbage plants without any great difficulty and it is also fairly easy to find Orange-tip eggs along country lanes in May, where the butterflies are seen on the wing. The eggs, especially in their orange stage, are clearly visible on the flower-heads of Jack-by-the-hedge, if these are examined carefully. Brimstone butterflies always lay their pointed eggs on the leaves of buckthorn growing in the hedges, and sometimes a number can be found by careful searching of the bushes. Where most butterflies are concerned, however, the capture of fertile females, or the collecting of caterpillars, are better methods.

The great advantage of starting with either eggs or with fertile females which are induced to lay in captivity, is that one can be sure that the caterpillars will not be parasitized. Larvae collected 'wild' are often badly 'stung' although they may appear quite healthy in the early stages.

Caterpillars

Certain butterfly caterpillars are very easy to find and this applies especially to those which are gregarious. 'Nests' of Small Tortoise-shell and Peacock larvae can be found without any difficulty on nettle beds, where they spin conspicuous webs of silk round the tops of the plants. Nettle beds in the vicinity of farm buildings are the best hunting grounds for Tortoiseshells in the spring and the second brood larvae are more likely to be found on young nettles growing up where the beds have been cut early in the summer. The best way to collect these larvae is to put a fairly large paper bag underneath the nest and then cut off the nettles with scissors or secateurs so that the whole brood drops into the bag.

Larvae of Hairstreaks and Holly Blues are best collected by beating, using either a proper beating tray, or a sheet of some material to spread out under the branches or clumps of ivy. A beating tray is a piece of material, usually black or green, stretched on a framework which can be folded up when not in use. A large upturned umbrella can also be made to serve. The tray or sheet is held some little distance below the branch and this is then beaten smartly with a stick to dislodge the caterpillars which will fall down into the tray.

Caterpillars which feed under cover of darkness are most easily found at night, with the aid of a powerful torch, and once a collector 'gets his eye in' the larvae are not difficult to see. A sweeping net is a useful piece of apparatus for night collecting of larvae which feed on grass and other low plants. This is simply a small net, not more than a foot in diameter, fixed on a specially strong and rigid frame, with a bag of stout calico or other material that will not tear easily. The net is swept from side to side close to the ground so that larvae feeding there will be dislodged and caught in the bag.

Caterpillars of Fritillaries, which are fairly conspicuous, Painted Ladies, Red Admirals, Small Coppers and White Admirals can be found by careful searching in the right localities at the proper season. Folded and nibbled leaves and traces of excrement often give a clue to the whereabouts of feeding larvae.

Butterfly larvae should be kept confined, either in cages or in bags of muslin or organdie, to prevent them straying and also to protect them from attacks by parasitic flies which can easily gain access even to rooms and greenhouses. There are two entirely different methods of raising butterfly larvae. The old-fashioned way, which many breeders still prefer, is to keep the caterpillars under conditions as nearly natural as possible, preferably out of doors, or in a light, well-ventilated room on growing food. The other way is to keep them all the time in darkness and a temperature of between 60 and 80 degrees

F. as, for example, in an airing cupboard, and feed them on cut food, supplied fresh daily. Both methods are worth trying and the latter way certainly appears to speed up the rate of growth, as the larvae feed continuously and are not influenced by changes in the weather.

The two most important points to bear in mind when rearing caterpillars are to avoid overcrowding, especially with those species which are solitary by nature, and to keep the food fresh. Stale, withered or waterlogged food leads to disease, and so does over-crowding. The cages should be kept as clean as possible and the larvae should never be allowed to starve. Many caterpillars do very well 'sleeved' on growing food out of doors, and this applies especially to those which feed on trees or shrubs. The so-called 'sleeving' method is very simple. A piece of muslin of suitable size is sewn up in the shape of a wide tube or sleeve and slipped over a branch or twig. It is then tied securely at the lower end, round the branch, the caterpillars are put inside, and the other end is also tied up to prevent them crawling out. When most of the leaves on the branch have been eaten the sleeve is changed over on to a fresh limb. The caterpillars should not be handled if this can be avoided. A smart rap on the branch will usually dislodge them and the sleeve can then be untied at the lower end, slipped off with the caterpillars lying at the bottom, and put over a fresh twig where they will soon climb up and begin to feed again. The excrement collected in the sleeve must be emptied out at regular intervals, and if the weather turns very bad it is best to cut off the branch and bring it indoors to stand in water for a few days, transferring the larvae to a fresh branch of the tree when the rainy period is over.

Many larvae are easier to raise in captivity on a substitute food plant than on the food they normally eat in their natural state. Green-veined Whites, Large and Small Whites for example, will eat horse radish leaves and the two latter do not have such an unpleasant smell as they do when fed on cabbage. These leaves, being long and narrow, can also easily be slipped into small organdie sleeves, and when the food needs to be changed the stale leaf can be sandwiched in between two fresh ones in a moment, and all three slipped back into the bag, the stalk of the stale leaf being cut off so that it will wither quickly and induce the caterpillars to crawl over on to the fresh ones. The larvae of the Chalk-hill Blue, the Common Blue and the Green Hairstreak will do very well when feeding on fresh green peas, and the Comma will eat leaves of hop and wych elm as well as nettles. Any food given to caterpillars should always be dry and clean. If it is raining when the food is gathered, it should be allowed to dry off before being put in the cages, and if leaves are dusty or sooty they must be washed first, by swishing them round in a bucket of water and leaving them to dry.

Caterpillars which hibernate in a fairly advanced stage of growth should be left out of doors through the winter, exposed to the weather, but protected against birds and other enemies. A good supply of dry leaves will give them somewhere to hide and the cages should, if possible, be kept under some kind of roof to prevent them getting too wet. If the food plant is available through the winter and the larvae normally feed during mild spells, they can be kept indoors and will complete their metamorphosis earlier than they would in nature. Marsh Fritillaries can be woken from hibernation early and fed on honeysuckle, which comes into leaf in February; and by using completely artificial conditions of heat and darkness some butterflies – for example the Large White – can be bred continuously all the year round.

Chrysalids

Hunting for butterfly chrysalids is a thankless task which few entomologists undertake, because they are usually very difficult to find. Caterpillars reared in captivity should be left to pupate on the sides of their cages or amongst their food plants and the pupae should not be touched until they have become quite firm. Chrysalids which are attached by a silken pad and girdle should, whenever possible, be left in their natural positions as, unless the pupa is fixed, the butterfly may have great difficulty in pulling itself out of the shell when it emerges, and a high percentage of cripples will result. The same thing applies to those which hang suspended head downwards; they, however, can be detached with less risk. In the case of the Small Tortoiseshell and the Peacock, which can be seriously parasitized by chalcids, it is a wise precaution to put the fully fed caterpillars, which are ready to pupate, into cardboard boxes with close-fitting lids to prevent their being 'stung'. The flies are so small that they can get through mosquito netting or perforated zinc, but in boxes the pupae will be found suspended from the lid and perfectly safe from attack.

The best way of keeping overwintering pupae is to store them in metal tins or boxes, with close-fitting lids. They need not be packed in moss or cotton wool, but should simply be laid side by side on the bottom of the tin, and this should be stored in a cool place. Frost will in no way harm hibernating pupae. In the spring they are taken out of the tins and laid on damp moss in a cage, with plenty of twigs leaning up against the sides so that the butterflies can crawl upwards and dry their wings as soon as they emerge. It is possible to hurry the emergence of spring butterflies by putting the chrysalids in a warm place, such as an airing cupboard, but they must be sprayed with water daily, or the unnatural heat will dry them up and kill them.

When the butterflies emerge it is important to let them become completely dry before any of them are killed for the collection. If the wings are still soft and moist they are likely to be damaged or crinkle. They should not, however, be allowed to flutter about in the cage as this will cause damage very quickly. If the cage is kept in a dark place the insects are less likely to flap about. It is a wise policy to release any surplus butterflies which are not wanted for the collection or further breeding. The more widespread species can be released almost anywhere the locality seems suitable, but local butterflies are very unlikely to breed successfully away from their native area. Attempts to establish butterflies in fresh localities have been made many times but it takes a great number of insects and much perseverance to succeed.

Many collectors are especially interested in aberrations of butterflies, and by keeping a strain going for several years it is sometimes possible to breed varieties by carefully selecting the parents. Some butterflies are very difficult to breed, others very easy, and a few, which will not pair in captivity, are virtually impossible to carry on from one year to the next. The interest derived from such experiments, however, and the knowledge gained, is always worth the effort, and the pleasure of successful breeding outweighs the disappointments. Our knowledge of butterflies is as yet far from complete and anybody who breeds these insects in an intelligent manner and keeps records of his findings may very well discover something new.

Adult Butterflies

When setting out to capture fertile female butterflies, it is important to select a suitable time. The hibernating butterflies such as Brimstones and Small Tortoiseshells should not be taken too early in the spring because they will not yet have paired; any eggs they lay are likely to be infertile. Even with summer butterflies it is best to wait for some days after the insects have begun to emerge, as the males usually appear before the females. It is more or less useless to capture very worn old specimens, because if they are not completely laid out they will in any case lay very few eggs.

A female butterfly will not lay if it is simply shut up in a box or a cage indoors. Quite a lot of preparation is usually needed to induce it to deposit its eggs. With the exception of the Marbled White and the Ringlet, which will drop their eggs on the bottom of the cage, provided they are fed and the sun is shining, all other butterflies will only lay on the correct food-plant, or on pieces of bark or some artificial substance which resembles it. Often a butterfly will not lay at once, and one may have to wait quite a long time, so the question of keeping the food-plant in a fresh condition arises. The best solution to this problem is to have the plant growing in a pot whenever possible, and this means potting up suitable plants early in the spring in readiness for breeding.

Butterflies confined in a cage will always flutter about and damage their wings to a certain extent, and a square cage where the insects batter themselves in the corners is not really suitable as a laying cage, which should, if possible, be round. A cheese tub or a small barrel is ideal, covered with a piece of muslin or netting secured with a string round the top of the tub. Another kind of laying cage can be made by using a large flower pot, planted with the correct food plant and covered with netting draped over a couple of canes or pieces of bent wire, which have their ends pushed into the soil to make a dome-shaped foundation for the cover.

As well as the food-plant, either growing or standing in a bottle of water, the butterflies will need food in the shape of fresh nectar-bearing flowers. Alyssum, sweet rocket, valerian, ox-eye daisies and knapweed, flowering thistle and buddleia are best. To supplement the flowers it is a good idea to put a pad of cotton wool soaked in a sugar or honey solution, on top of the muslin of the cage, renewing it

25

daily. Sunshine is also absolutely essential, but the cage should not be stood for any length of time in the full heat of the sun or the butterflies will quickly die. Dappled sunlight is the ideal, or short spells in the full sun. The whole cage should be sprayed with water from a fine-rose watering can several times a day in warm weather, as this will give the insects the moisture they need to keep them alive.

All the Fritillaries, with the exception of the Heath and Marsh Fritillaries, can be induced to lay if the sides of the tub or cage are draped with muslin, netting or old lace curtains. The texture of these apparently deceives the insects and they will tuck their eggs into the materials. The Browns and most of the Skippers will lay on tussocks of grass potted up. Stinging nettles are suitable for the Vanessas, except the Painted Lady which prefers thistles. The Small Copper will lay on dock or sorrel leaves, and the Clouded Yellows on lucerne or clover. Wild primrose or polyanthus is suitable for the Duke of Burgundy Fritillary, devil's-bit scabious for the Marsh Fritillary, and narrow leaved plantain for the Heath Fritillary. All these plants can easily be grown in pots.

When it is noticed that the butterflies have begun to lay, the food-plant should be examined every evening. If there are a number of eggs on the leaves it should be taken out of the cage and a fresh plant put in instead, because if too many eggs are laid on one plant the young caterpillars will be overcrowded as soon as they hatch. In the case of butterflies whose larvae are cannibals in the early stages, this is particularly important, and it is best to cut off the eggs and distribute them on a number of plants just before they hatch. The Orange-tip is a case in point, and the best way to rear it is to have many separate bottles, each one with a single piece of food-plant, so that the larvae have no chance of attacking each other.

When the eggs have been laid on a growing plant there is no need to touch them or store them away. All that is necessary is to keep the plant watered and see that it stands in a place where earwigs, spiders, aphids and other creatures cannot get at it and eat the eggs. A good way of getting rid of pests which may be hiding in the soil or among the low stems of the plants is to immerse the whole pot in a bucket of water and leave it there for twenty minutes or so, moving it about once or twice to dislodge any clinging creatures, which will then float up to the surface. The plant should then be well drained before being put in the laying cage.

When eggs are laid on cut food which will not keep fresh, each bottle should be dated, so that it is possible to calculate fairly accurately when the eggs will hatch. The twig or spray can then be stood between fresh pieces and the young larvae will quickly move over from the withered food to the fresh. Eggs laid on green leaves should not be stored in air-tight tins or boxes, but this is a good method for keeping the eggs of Fritillaries, laid on muslin, as it prevents them or the very young hibernating larvae from drying up during the winter.

BUTTERFLIES IN BRITAIN

Butterflies belong to the superfamily Rhopalocera and together with moths are included in the order Lepidoptera. The sixty-eight species classed as British, although several are rare immigrants only, are again divided into eight families and a number of genera. A brief account of the characteristics of each respective family is given further on in this book.

Nearly all the British butterflies have their own favourite type of locality and are only found in the kind of country which suits their particular requirements. The southern half of Britain is richer in butterflies than the northern and eastern counties and Scotland, but a few species, such as the Scotch Argus and the Mountain Ringlet, are found only in the north, while the handsome Swallow-tail is now confined to the Norfolk Broads area.

As butterflies can only feed on nectar they are nearly always attracted by flowers, and many of them are often seen in gardens, especially in the spring, and again when the buddleia bushes are in bloom and in the autumn when the Michaelmas-daisies come into flower. Small Tortoiseshells and Peacocks are the most common of the garden visitors and it is easy to watch them at close quarters when they are busily feeding. The Red Admiral and the Painted Lady, both migrants, often come into gardens, and those two garden pests, the Large White and the Small White, always keep to gardens or cultivated places where they can find the cabbages on which their caterpillars feed.

Country lanes and fields, where plenty of wild flowers grow in the hedgerows, and many different plants and shrubs provide food for the larvae, are good places for observing butterflies. In the spring, Orange-tips, Green-veined Whites and Brimstones fly along the hedges, and later on in the summer the Small Copper, the Meadow Brown, Hedge Brown and several of the various Skippers can be seen. The Clouded Yellow and the Pale Clouded Yellow, both migrants, gather in lucerne and clover fields and one may come across little colonies of the Common Blue in rough fields.

Woodland butterflies are quite distinct from those of the open country and like the shelter of trees. They do not, however, fly in the densely wooded and dark parts of a forest, but prefer the open ridings and sunny glades where they can find flowers. Several of the Fritillaries are typical woodland insects. In the early summer the Pearl-bordered and the Small Pearl-bordered Fritillaries are on the wing and later on the Heath Fritillary, the High Brown Fritillary and the Silver-washed Fritillary. The White Admiral is another typical woodland insect and so is the Purple Emperor. All the Hairstreaks, except the Green Hairstreak, which prefers more open country, are found in woods, and the Speckled Wood and the Wood White are also true to their names in their choice of locality. The Comma butterfly breeds and hibernates in woodlands, but sometimes visits gardens like the other Vanessa butterflies.

The downs of southern England are typical Blue butterfly country and all the members of this family of insects, except the Holly Blue which prefers the edges of woods or parks and gardens, fly on open windswept hills. The Dark Green Fritillary, the Marsh Fritillary and the Small Heath also frequent open downland or heaths. The Marbled White is another butterfly that likes sunny high ground, while the Large Heath is found in peat-bogs in a few areas from Shropshire northwards. A few butterflies are found mainly near the coast, and one of these is the Lulworth Skipper. The Essex Skipper and the Large Blue are also found near the sea, and the Grayling is common in some coastal areas. Some butterflies have a very restricted range and do not spread to other areas even though conditions there may appear to be suitable, while others are widely distributed and can be found in many different places.

The distribution of butterflies does not remain constant and over the years gradual changes take place, some species becoming more rare and restricted, while others increase and spread. During this century the butterfly population as a whole has decreased, mainly because of the spread of towns and increased urbanization, the draining of land, felling of woods and atmospheric pollution. But although some butterflies have become so rare that they are in danger of extinction, like the Large Blue, the Glanville Fritillary and the Swallowtail, others have become much more common and widespread than they used to be. The Comma and the White Admiral increased in numbers and extended their range about forty years ago, but both have since decreased in many areas.

Every year the migrating butterflies which come over from the Continent increase our native population. Sometimes they arrive in enormous numbers; in other years comparatively few reach our shores. Migrations often begin quite early in the summer and may continue until autumn, and the migrants breed in this country, producing a second and even a third generation of butterflies. The spring migration is always in a northerly direction, but in the autumn the migrant butterflies begin to fly towards the south again and many of them leave England, just as migrant birds do, often flying at night.

The habits and behaviour of the different butterflies vary a great deal, and it is only by studying them in their haunts that one can learn much about the living insects, and the way in which they differ from each other. The behaviour of the males is usually quite distinct from that of the females, which as soon as they have mated begin to search for the correct food plant on which to lay their eggs.

On their first flight most newly emerged butterflies look for flowers, and begin to feed on nectar, but very soon the males begin searching for the females. Butterflies find each other mainly by sight, but in some species the female also gives out a scent by which the male can track her down if she is not visible. These scents cannot be detected by the human nose, but the male scents, the function of which is to stimulate the female during courtship, can in some cases be distinguished by people who have a good sense of smell. The Green-veined White, for example, smells fairly strongly of lemon verbena, but in many other species the smell is quite faint. The scales which give off the scent are usually clearly visible on the fore-wings of the males in the shape of dark bands known as androconia.

The courtship of butterflies varies with the species. Before mating the male and female often perform intricate courtship flights, chasing each other backwards and forwards over the same piece of ground, or rising steeply in spiral flight until they are almost out of sight. If the female is sitting still the male will often walk round her, touching her body and wings with his antennae, or hover above her to scatter his scent. The actual pairing may last for several hours, or in some species no more than fifteen minutes or so. If the butterflies are disturbed while pairing they will take to the wing, still joined, one carrying the other. Sometimes the male carries the female, but in many cases it is the female that carries the male.

The life span of butterflies can be long or short, but is never as brief as is popularly supposed. Even the smallest and most fragile of our butterflies can live a fortnight, provided weather conditions are good and they are able to fly and feed. Cold rainy weather naturally shortens their life. The hibernating butterflies are very long lived. Peacocks and Brimstones often survive for ten or eleven months.

Throughout their life span, both as butterflies and in their various other stages, these insects have many enemies. Birds chase and catch butterflies as well as innumerable caterpillars and chrysalids. Wasps also attack larvae and carry them off for feeding their grubs in the nests, and solitary wasps paralyse many caterpillars and store them as food for their own offspring. The most deadly enemies of butterflies, however, are the parasites which attack them during their early stages. These are insects of the orders Hymenoptera, known as ichneumon-flies, and Diptera which lay their eggs on the skin, or inside the body of a caterpillar. In doing this ichneumon-flies pierce the skin of the victims with their long ovipositors. The eggs hatch inside the caterpillars and develop into grubs which feed on the internal tissues of their hosts until they are killed. Sometimes the eggs are not laid on the host itself but close by it, on the leaves of the food plant, so that they are sure to be eaten, or else the young grubs, on hatching, bore their way into the body of the host.

The very small chalcid flies attack the chrysalids, often waiting beside a caterpillar for the change to take place. Parasites greatly reduce the numbers of caterpillars and have sometimes been responsible for the complete disappearance of butterflies from certain localities. Earwigs, spiders, mice and shrews also take a toll of caterpillars, chrysalids and eggs.

DESCRIPTIONS

MILKWEED or MONARCH *Danaus plexippus* Pl. 1

Description. Wing-span: 3½ in. Sexes similar. Ground colour rich reddish-brown with black veinings and wide marginal bands enclosing a double row of white spots. The male has a patch of black scent scales on each hind-wing. Underside pattern similar but the ground colour on the hind-wings is buff and the black veining very pronounced.

Length of life. 8–9 months.

Distribution. A rare visitor from America. First recorded in Britain in 1876, and since that year about two hundred examples have been reported, mainly in the south-west of England and Ireland.

Habitat. Cliff-sides, on arrival, or inland parks and gardens, to which it would be attracted by flowers for nectar.

Habits. Powerful flight, soaring and gliding on the wind currents like a sea-bird; has immense reserves of strength.

Life history. *Eggs*: pale yellow, laid singly on the leaves of milk-weed. Hatch in three or four days. *Caterpillar*: 2¼ in. Pale greenish-yellow striped alternately in black and white. There is a pair of long black horns, pointing forwards behind the head, and another pair, considerably shorter and facing in the other direction, are situated near the tail end of the body. *Chrysalis*: almost cylindrical in shape and smoothly rounded at the end, a clear jade green encircled by a golden band and studded with gilded points. Hangs suspended from a pad of silk attached to a leaf-stalk. *Butterfly*: winters in a state of semi-hibernation, in Florida in the east, and California in the west of the USA. In the spring the butterflies move north, laying eggs and colonizing the countryside as they go, until they die of old age. Brood succeeds brood and as autumn approaches the butterflies band together and begin to move south again to their winter quarters. Occasionally some specimens appear to stray off course, cross the Atlantic on their own wing power or as involuntary stowaways on board cargo ships, arriving on our coastline during the autumn months. As milkweed, the food-plant of the caterpillars, does not grow in Britain, there is no chance of the species becoming established here.

Plate 1

1 Milkweed, *Danaus plexippus* (p. 35) ♂ (sexes similar) × ⅔
1a underside ♂ × ⅔

2 Scotch Argus, *Erebia aethiops* (p. 41) ♂ (sexes differ slightly)
2a underside ♂
2b ♀
2c ab. *ochracea* Mousley variety; underside

3 Mountain Ringlet, *Erebia epiphron* (p. 40) ♂ (sexes very similar)
3a underside ♂
3b ♀

4 Speckled Wood, *Pararge aegeria* (p. 39) ♂ (sexes differ slightly)
4a underside ♂
4b ♀

5 Wall Brown, *Lasiommata megera* (p. 38) ♂ (sexes differ)
5a underside ♂
5b ♀
5c ♂ ab. *mediolugens* Fuchs
5d ♀ ab. *mediolugens* Fuchs
5e ♀ ab. *quadriocellata* Oberthur

Scale: All life size except where otherwise indicated.

With the exception of the Milkweed, which is an occasional American vagrant, all the butterflies on this plate are members of the Brown family. They feed in the caterpillar stage on various grasses and spend the winter in hibernation as small caterpillars. The Mountain Ringlet and Scotch Argus are found only in the North of England and in Scotland, whereas the other two, the Wall Brown and the Speckled Wood are very widely distributed. The Browns do not vary to any great extent, but occasionally specimens differ from the normal in their ground colouring or in the number of spots on their wings (figs. 5c, 5d and 5e). The spring brood of the Speckled Wood has more and larger light markings than the summer form.

36

Plate 2

1 Marbled White, *Melanargia galathea* (p. 42) ♂ (sexes differ slightly)
1a underside ♂
1b ♀

2 Grayling, *Hipparchia semele* (p. 43) ♂ (sexes differ)
2a underside ♂
2b ♀

3 Hedge Brown, *Pyronia tithonus* (p. 46) ♂ (sexes differ slightly)
3a underside ♂
3b ♀
3c ♀ ab. *pallescens* Cockerell
3d ♂ ab. *multiocellata* Oberthur

4 Meadow Brown, *Maniola jurtina* (p. 47) ♂ (sexes differ)
4a underside ♂
4b ♀
4c ♀ ab. *grisea-aurea* Oberthur

Scale: All butterflies on this plate are life size.

This plate consists entirely of the Brown family, even though one of them, the Marbled White, would appear, by its name, to belong to the Whites. All the caterpillars are grass feeders, and spend the winter in this stage in hibernation. The Grayling varies greatly according to the localities where it breeds, and there are two named sub-species, one a dwarf race found in Wales, Welsh subsp. *thyone* and another, very richly coloured, in Ireland, Irish subsp. *atlantica*. The Hedge Brown and the Meadow Brown both throw lovely coloured varieties (fig. 3c) and albino forms occur very occasionally (fig. 4c). The Hedge Brown has a strong tendency towards extra spotting on both fore- and hind-wings, especially the forms found in Devon and Cornwall (fig. 3d).

WALL BROWN *Lasiommata megera* Pl. 1

Description. Wing-span: 1¾ in. Sexes differ. Ground colour of male bright tawny-brown. A thick band of dark scent scales runs across the fore-wing from the centre to the hind margin. There are three short dark bars at the front edge and a curved line between the scent scales and the outer margin, which is bordered with a chocolate band. Near the tip there is a small white-centred eye-spot. Hindwings brown near the body, rest of the wing bright tawny-brown with a row of eye-spots running parallel to the margin. Female slightly larger with lighter yellowish-brown ground colour; the spots on the hind-wings are always more prominent than in the male, and edged with a scalloped brown line. Underside markings correspond to the upperside on the fore-wings, hind-wings mottled in grey, brown and buff, marked with zigzag brown lines and seven dark-centred eye-spots. Plate 1: fig. 5c ab. *mediolugens* male; fig. 5d ab. *mediolugens* female, banded forms, not uncommon; fig. 5e ab. *quadriocellata*, four-spotted form. Markings and spotting vary considerably.

Length of life. 12–16 days.

Distribution. Common and widespread in England, Wales, and a limited part of southern Scotland. Also found in many parts of Ireland.

Habitat. Uncultivated waste-land, heaths and commons, country lanes and hillsides.

Habits. Quick restless flight, never settling long anywhere; frequently alights on the bare ground and rests with wings open.

Life history. *Eggs*: greenish-white, laid singly on blades of various common grasses. *Caterpillar*: 1 in. Bluish-green, with a dark green band down the back, edged with white lines; three indistinct pale green lines run along the sides of the body, and a white stripe below the yellow spiracles. Body is covered with small warts and short downy hairs. Overwinters in a grass tussock, feeding intermittently in mild weather. *Chrysalis*: rather short and rounded, with two rows of white points and a rather rough surface. Usually bright grass green, but sometimes dark brown or nearly black. Hangs from a grass blade, the anal hooks caught in a pad of silk on the flat surface. *Butterfly*: first brood emerges in mid-May, second on the wing from late in July, during August and the early part of September.

SPECKLED WOOD   *Pararge aegeria*   Pl. 1

Description.   Wing-span: 1¾ in. Sexes differ slightly. Male with blackish-brown ground colour, fore-wings marked with eleven yellowish blotches and a small black-ringed white eye-spot near the tip. Hind-wings carry two straw-coloured marks near the front edge and a chain of three eye-spots along the margin which is slightly scalloped. Female has more rounded wings, is slightly larger with lighter ground colour; markings resemble those of the male, but are larger and bolder. Underside almost identical in both sexes; fore-wings with pale ground and well-defined black markings and eye-spot at the tip, hind-wings mottled with deep buff and brown with a greyish-mauve band along the margin and a row of five eye-spots.

Length of life.   12–16 days.

Distribution.   Common locally in much of southern England and Ireland, also found in smaller numbers in northern England, Wales, north-west Scotland.

Habitat.   Woodland glades and pathways, shady country lanes, outskirts of wooded country.

Habits.   Weak flitting flight along sunlit pathways and in the shadow of overhanging trees in woodland glades. Sit with wings wide open on grass blades, sunning themselves.

Life history.   *Eggs*: creamy-white, laid singly on blades of various grasses. *Caterpillar*: 1 in. Grass green, with a darker green line along the centre of the back, edged with yellowish-green. Skin covered with minute white warts carrying short greyish silky hairs. *Chrysalis*: colour varies from bright green to dark greenish-brown; short and blunt with two small points on the head. Hangs suspended from a grass blade by hooks attached to a pad of silk. Can either spend the winter in the chrysalis stage, or as a hibernating caterpillar in a grass tussock, depending upon how late in the summer the female butterfly laid her last eggs. *Butterfly*: first ones emerge in April, and from then onwards until late in June. Second broods begin appearing in early August and are on the wing until the end of September, or into October in a hot dry summer.

MOUNTAIN RINGLET   *Erebia epiphron*   Pl. 1

Description. Wing-span: $1\frac{1}{4}$ in. Sexes very similar. Males dark chocolate-brown, with a wide light brown band running across the fore-wings parallel with the margin; across this band the veins are marked in dark brown and in each space there is a black dot. Hind-wings marked with four light brown blotches, also dotted with black, and forming a curved chain. The females have rather larger spots in slightly wider bands. Undersides marked in a similar way, but the ground colour is a lighter brown and the spotting not so prominent and may be partially absent.

Length of life. 10–14 days.

Distribution. A very local northern species. A few colonies in the English Lake District, and others in the Scottish Highlands. No recent Irish records. Not usually seen below 1500 ft.

Habitat. High on mountains, usually in swampy hollows, often near small streams.

Habits. Flies low over the ground, and instantly drops on to the grass if a cloud obscures the sun. Rests with wings closed and is difficult to find except in sunny weather.

Life history. *Eggs*: yellow, turning to rust-red before hatching; laid singly in blades of mat grass. *Caterpillar*: just under $\frac{3}{4}$ in. Green, with a darker green line along the centre of the back, edged on either side with white; alternate stripes of green and white down the length of the body. Rough skin covered with small black points. Overwinters hidden in a clump of grass. Pupates in a flimsy cocoon down among the grass stems, drawing a few blades together with strands of silk. *Chrysalis*: colour varies from light green to pale cream, speckled and streaked with brown. *Butterfly*: emerges in mid-June and flies until the second or third week in July.

SCOTCH ARGUS *Erebia aethiops* Pl. 1

Description. Wing-span: 1½ in. Sexes differ slightly. Male dark-brown with a reddish-brown band near the margin of the fore-wings in which are set three white-centred, black eye-spots; hind-wings carry three more similar spots encircled by reddish-brown. Female markings similar but spotting always bolder and ground colour slightly lighter brown. Underside pattern and markings similar in both sexes; the wide band on the hind-wings is pearly-grey in the male and yellowish-brown in the female.

Length of life. 14–18 days.

Distribution. Found locally in north-west England, and more widely in Scotland. Now extinct in Yorkshire, and not found in Ireland.

Habitat. On the sides of mountains and hills, and in valleys, but never at a great altitude.

Habits. Slow fluttering flight over the grass, settling with wings closed as soon as the sun goes in.

Life history. *Eggs*: pale yellow, laid singly on blades of blue moor grass. Become spotted with violet in two or three days and turn greyish-purple before hatching. *Caterpillar*: Just under 1 in. Light yellow with a slightly raised brown stripe along the back, becoming darker and wider towards the tail end. The sides are marked with a chequered pale purplish-brown line and beneath this is another line of dull greenish-brown edged with creamy-white. Hibernates in a tussock of grass and begins feeding in March on blue moor grass. Pupates on the ground in a flimsy silken cocoon. *Chrysalis*: light cream with a greyish suffusion across the wing-cases and three brown lines across the back. *Butterfly*: emerges about the end of July and is on the wing for most of August.

MARBLED WHITE   *Melanargia galathea*   Pl. 2

Description.   Wing-span: male 1¾ in., female 2 in. Sexes differ slightly. Ground colour creamy-white or pale yellow, all four wings are marked with irregular black squares and blotches alternating with about an equal number of light areas. On the hind-wings there are two or three rather faint eye-spots, set in a scalloped black band. The female is always a slightly larger butterfly with more pale areas and enlarged hind-wing eye-spots. Underside pattern corresponds to upperside, hind-wings always paler, especially in the female which has a definite creamy-yellow tint, and the spots are well defined.

Length of life.   14–18 days.

Distribution.   Found mainly, and in some places commonly, in southern and south-west England, but extends to east Yorkshire. Often on limestone or chalk, but not confined to these.

Habitat.   On the chalk and limestone downs of southern England, rough hillsides, and occasionally in uncultivated fields.

Habits.   Slow floppy flight just above the grasses, frequently settling on wild flowers or grass stems, basking in the sun with wings wide open.

Life history.   *Eggs*: white, dropped as the female flies low over the grass.   *Caterpillar*: just over 1 in. Colour varies from creamy-yellow to pale green. A dark line runs down the centre of the back bordered on each side by a white line. Alternate faint bands of pale violet and pink, separated by white lines, run the length of the body. Short white hairs growing from warts cover body and head and give the caterpillar a silky appearance. Hibernates as a minute caterpillar low down among the grass immediately after eating its egg-shell. Begins to feed in mild spells any time after Christmas, but matures very slowly. Pupates on the ground without any covering, usually at the base of a grass tussock.   *Chrysalis*: creamy-yellow, flushed with pink, often speckled with brown.   *Butterfly*: does not emerge until the middle of July, on the wing for most of August.

Description. Wing-span: male 2 in., female 2¼ in. Sexes differ. Ground colour of male bronze-brown; fore-wings carry two dark-ringed eye-spots surrounded by a suffusion of light brown and a sloping band of androconial scent scales. Hind-wings have a broad fulvous band crossed by dark veins and a single eye-spot; margins slightly scalloped. Ground colour of female lighter, with well-defined yellow and brown bands edged by wavy black border; eye-spots near the tip larger than in the male. Band on hind-wings usually lighter and broader. Underside markings, fore-wings light brownish-yellow at base, pale straw coloured on outer half with a dark brown bar and two prominent eye-spots. Hind-wings mottled and streaked with black and brown, with a broad white band running across the wing outlined in black.

Length of life. 16–21 days.

Distribution. Locally in suitable areas in much of Britain including north-west Scotland, more local in Ireland. A small race is found in north Wales.

Habitat. Commons and heaths, rocky hillsides and downland, also by the seaside on rocky coasts.

Habits. Takes advantage of its camouflage markings and strong resemblance to grey lichen by usually settling on weather-beaten rocks or bare soil, with the fore-wings tucked down out of sight so that the tell-tale eye-spot on the tip of each fore-wing is hidden. Always sits at an angle to the ground to avoid casting any shadow; fast vigorous flight over short distances, frequently settling, always with wings tightly closed.

Life history. *Eggs*: white, laid singly, glued by the female to blades of grass. *Caterpillar*: 1¾ in. Light yellow, with five drab-coloured longitudinal lines; the body slim, narrowing towards the tail which ends in two points, densely covered with pale hair. Hibernates deep in a grass tussock. Pupates underground, burrowing out a small chamber about half an inch deep in the soil. *Chrysalis*: plump and rounded, reddish-brown, devoid of all markings except two rough black projections on either side. *Butterfly*: emerges in mid-July and on the wing during August; sometimes still flying in early September.

Plate 3

1 **Small Pearl-bordered Fritillary**, *Clossiana selene* (p. 51) ♂ (sexes very similar)
1a underside ♂. 1b ♀
1c ♂, extreme aberration, unnamed
1d ♂ ab. *pallida* Spoler
1e ♂ ab. *extennata* Cabean (extreme)

2 **Queen of Spain Fritillary**, *Issoria lathonia* (p. 55) ♂ (sexes similar). 2a underside ♂

3 **Small Heath**, *Coenonympha pamphilus* (p. 50) ♂ (sexes differ slightly). 3a underside ♂

4 **Large Heath**, *Coenonympha tullia* (p. 49) ♂ (sexes differ)
4a underside ♂. 4b ♀
4c ♂ subsp. *scotica* Stgr.
4d underside ♂ subsp. *scotica* Stgr.
4e ♀ subsp. *scotica* Stgr.

5 **Ringlet**, *Aphantopus hyperanthus* (p. 48) ♂ (sexes differ slightly)
5a underside ♂
5b ab. *caeca*
5c ab. *lanceolata*

Scale: All the butterflies on this plate are life size.

The Ringlet and the Small and Large Heath complete the family of Brown butterflies; other members are illustrated on plates 1 and 2. The Ringlet tends to extremes of variation in the spotting on the underside, and the eye-spots may be reduced to mere pin-points (fig. 5b) or enlarged to pear-shaped spots heavily ringed with yellow (fig. 5c). The Small Heath remains constant wherever it is found in the British Isles, but the Large Heath is extremely variable, and two distinct sub-species are named, the Scottish one being very pale in colour and lightly spotted, whereas the other form is very heavily spotted. The Small Pearl-Bordered Fritillary is given to considerable variation in the form of changes of wing pattern or ground colours (figs. 1c, 1d and 1e); albino and dark melanic forms appear in some years.

Plate 4

1 Dark Green Fritillary, *Mesoacidalia aglaja* (p. 56) ♂ (sexes differ slightly) × ⅔
1a underside ♂ × ⅔
1b ♀ × ⅔

2 High Brown Fritillary, *Fabriciana adippe* (p. 57) ♂ (sexes differ slightly) × ⅔
2a underside ♂ × ⅔
2b ♀ × ⅔

3 Silver-washed Fritillary, *Argynnis paphia* (p. 58) ♂ (sexes differ) × ⅔
3a underside ♂ × ⅔
3b ♀ × ⅔
3c ab. *valesina* Esper. ♀ × ⅔

4 Pearl-bordered Fritillary, *Clossiana euphrosyne* (p. 54) ♀ (sexes very similar)
4a underside ♀
4b ♂
4c extreme ab. near *nigricans* Oberthur

Scale: All life-size except where otherwise indicated.

The Fritillary family consists of mostly, but not exclusively, wood-land insects. They pass the winter either in the egg stage, or hiber-nating as small caterpillars; the most usual food-plant is the dog violet. All the butterflies illustrated on this plate feed in the caterpillar stage on violets. The Silver-washed and Pearl-bordered Fritillaries will be found in woodland glades and ridings, but the High Brown often strays into fields and heathland in the vicinity of wooded country. The Dark Green Fritillary is a fast-flying butterfly of the windswept downs and hillsides, or rough uncultivated meadows. All four species are much given to extreme forms of variation, ranging from colour forms to albino and melanic insects (fig. 4c).

45

HEDGE BROWN or GATEKEEPER *Pyronia tithonus*

Pl. 2

Description.   Wing-span: male 1½ in., female 1⅝ in. Sexes differ slightly. Male: ground colour rich golden-brown with fore-wings broadly edged with dusky-brown, and a wide brown streak carrying scent scales extending from the front edge to near the centre. Near the tip is a white-centred double eye-spot. Hind-wings surrounded by a wide dark band, central areas golden-brown, with one or two small eye-spots on the edge of the band. Female lighter in colour and without the streak on the fore-wings, and is slightly larger in size. Underside similar in both sexes, except that the female is always rather paler in colour. Fore-wings resemble upperside; hind-wings brown with a wide straw-coloured band with irregular wavy edges, carrying a number of white spots surrounded by light tawny areas. Plate 2: fig. 3c, colour form ab. *pallescens*; fig. 3d, male with extra spots on fore- and hind-wings, ab. *multiocellata*, not uncommon in Devon and Cornwall.

Length of life.   12–16 days.

Distribution.   Widespread and common in much of England, especially in the south and south-west, also in Wales but absent from Scotland. Limited to south and south-east Ireland.

Habitat.   Flies in country lanes, along the margins of fields bordered by hedges, and along woodland rides and pathways.

Habits.   This butterfly haunts hedgerows, feeding avidly on bramble blossom. Rather weak fluttery flight, often seeming to go round in circles and returning to the same spray of flowers or favourite leaf. Rests with wings closed.

Life history.   *Eggs:* yellow, laid singly in grass blades. *Caterpillar*: just under 1 in. Varies in colour from light green to yellowish-buff with a dark brown streak along the back and dark chocolate streaks and lines along the sides. The body, including the head, is covered with short, white bristly hairs. Hibernates over winter in a grass tussock, starting to feed again in March. *Chrysalis*: dingy-white, streaked and blotched with dark brown marks. Short and thick, and hangs suspended, attached to its cast larval skin, from a grass blade.   *Butterfly*: the first emerges in late July and emergence continues for a long time. On the wing during August and the early part of September.

MEADOW BROWN *Maniola jurtina* Pl. 2

Description. Wing-span: male 1¾ in., female 2 in. Sexes differ. Male dark brown with a small white-centred black eye-spot near the tip of the fore-wing. Below this is a small area of ginger-brown and a patch of dark scent scales running across the wing. Hind-wings similar in colour but often speckled with darker brown. Female has a larger ginger patch covering most of the outer fore-wing and near the tip is a large white-pupilled black spot; hind-wings have a corresponding lighter patch on a dark ground. Underside of both sexes a light brown with a paler wide band, edged with a wavy brown line, running across all four wings. There is the characteristic eye-spot at the tip of the fore-wings. Plate 2: fig. 4c, ab. *grisea-aurea*, a type of albino occasionally encountered in the field.

Length of life. 14–18 days.

Distribution. Found in much of Britain and Ireland and often common, but less so in many areas than formerly.

Habitat. Widespread, in fields and meadows, commons and heaths, hills and downland, woodland glades and ridings, and along country lanes. Not found in towns and on high moors.

Habits. Slow floppy flight, loath to take off from the ground or flower-head on which it may be resting. Flies in dull sunless weather, never straying far from the home area.

Life history. *Eggs*: pale yellow, laid singly on blades of grass. Become mottled with reddish-brown, and turn grey before hatching. *Caterpillar*: 1 in. Grass green, the upper surface paler than the lower, the two colours separated by a diffused white line. A dark green stripe runs along the back and the body is covered with fine greyish hair. Overwinters in a grass tussock, feeding on mild days after dusk. *Chrysalis*: grass green, speckled with yellow and marked with dark irregular lines on the wing cases. Attached to the old larval skin, it hangs from a blade of grass, the anal hooks caught in a pad of silk. *Butterfly*: emerges late June and early July, and may be seen until late September if the weather is very warm.

Description. Wing-span: 1¾ in. Sexes differ slightly. Male dull velvety-brown with two or three small eye-spots in the middle of fore- and hind-wing. The fringes are conspicuously white. Female similar markings but spots considerably larger than in the male, and ground colour a lighter shade of brown. Underside a somewhat lighter shade of brown, fore-wing carrying two or three spots, hind-wing usually five, all of them boldly ringed with light yellow. Plate 3: fig. 5b, ab. *caeca*, white dots instead of eye-spots; fig. 5c, ab. *lanceolata*, with spots enlarged and elongated. Underside markings very variable generally.

Length of life. 12–16 days.

Distribution. Local, but common in many areas in England and Wales. Less common in south Scotland, and widespread, though local, in Ireland.

Habitat. Primarily a woodland insect, but met with in country lanes bordered by hedgerows and on heaths and commons where copses form part of the landscape.

Habits. Will fly in dull weather, even slight rain. Slow flapping flight, always around bushes or trees, frequently settling to rest. Haunts tangles of bramble blossom, searching for nectar.

Life history. *Eggs*: yellow, dropped in the grass as the female flies along. Darken to grey-buff before hatching. *Caterpillar*: just under 1 in. Yellowish-buff with a rather darker line along the back and short streaks of dull pink all over the body. There is a row of dark spots along the sides and the entire surface is covered with short hairs. Feeds only at night but rests fully exposed on a blade of grass during the day. Overwinters in partial hibernation, feeding intermittently on mild days. Pupates in late June at the base of grass tussocks, in a network of silken threads. *Chrysalis*: yellowish, flushed with pink and marked all over with fine brown lines. Very rough surface. *Butterfly*: on the wing in the latter part of July and the first half of August.

Description. Wing-span: $1\frac{1}{4}$ in. Sexes differ. Male fore-wings dull brown merging into rusty-brown towards the base; black spot ringed with buff near the tip, and below this is a smaller one. Hind-wings rather darker shade with three buff-ringed dark spots near the margin. The female much lighter coloured, buff-brown, and the spots often more pronounced, with a light cream patch near the centre of the hind-wings. Underside of both sexes similar, but the eye-spot on the fore-wings and the chain of spots on the hind-wings smaller in the male than in the female; hind-wings covered with grey hairy scales, and a wide broken cream band cuts across both upper and lower wings, decorated with a chain of white-pupilled black spots ringed with cream. Plate 3: fig. 4c, subsp. *scotica*, male; fig. 4d, underside of same form; fig. 4e, upperside of same form, female, all from Scotland. A very variable species, each county having its own special form.

Length of life. 14–18 days.

Distribution. Found locally in peat areas of several counties of England north of Shropshire, but its numbers have declined seriously in recent years. Now uncommon in Wales, but more widespread, though not common, in Scotland and Ireland.

Habitat. On moorland, bogs and mosses.

Habits. Flies very close to the ground, zig-zagging backwards and forwards in boggy places.

Life history. *Eggs*: whitish-yellow, later turning straw coloured with brown blotches, laid singly on the leaves or stems of beaked rush. *Caterpillar*: clear green with a darker green line down the back and four wide white stripes running the length of the body. Tail has two pink and white points. Skin rough and covered with fine white hair. Hibernates over winter in a grass tussock, beginning to feed in early March. *Chrysalis*: bright green, speckled with brown pad of silk. *Butterfly*: emerges in mid-June and on the wing until the middle of July.

Description. Wing-span: 1 in. Sexes differ slightly. Male: light golden-brown ground colour, wings suffused with grey at the base. Fore-wing carries a small black spot near the tip and the margins are edged with greyish-brown; fringes light cream. Female slightly larger, with ground colour more yellowish-brown and the marginal bands much narrower. Underside similar in both sexes: fore-wings orange-brown with a light greyish blotch surrounding a white-centred eye-spot near the tip. Hind-wings grey on the basal half, thickly covered with greyish hairs, outer half much paler grey with a row of indistinct grey light-centred spots following the margin.

Length of life. 14–18 days.

Distribution. Common and widely distributed in Britain and Ireland, though more restricted in the latter country. In some areas its numbers have fallen in recent years because of the destruction of its grassy haunts.

Habitat. Waste-ground, fields and meadows, commons and heaths, hillsides, downs and mountains.

Habits. Slow flitting flight just above the grass, never roaming far from its home locality. Rests and feeds with wings closed.

Life history. *Eggs*: light green, laid singly on blades of grass. They become spotted with brown and turn almost transparent before hatching. *Caterpillar*: ¾ in. Yellowish-green, with three dark green lines along the back, all edged with white lines, and a wide band of dark green running along the spiracles. Rough skin covered with numerous white warts each sprouting short curved spine-like hairs. Overwinters half-grown, hibernating in a tussock of grass and feeding in mild weather. Pupates in late April. *Chrysalis*: pale green speckled with a darker green and two rows of white points on the abdomen; hangs from a blade of grass, attached by hooks at its tail end to a pad of silk. *Butterfly*: first brood emerges in May; second brood on the wing from mid-July until early in September.

SMALL PEARL-BORDERED FRITILLARY

Clossiana selene **Pl. 3**

Description. Wing-span: 1½ in. Sexes differ only slightly. Ground colour rich golden-brown, marked and spotted with black in a similar pattern to the Pearl-bordered Fritillary. Female always a rather darker insect with a cloudy suffusion of dark scaling at the base of the wings. Underside quite distinct from the Pearl-bordered Fritillary in having additional silver spots on the hind-wings and the red blotches deeper in colour and boldly outlined in black; a chain of small black spots runs in a curve parallel to the margin, often partially obscured by the blotches. Plate 3: fig. 1c, an extreme aberration, partially melanic; fig. 1d, ab. *pallida*, ground colour lemonish-straw; fig. 1e, ab. *extennata*, a male lacking most of the normal black markings.

Length of life. 14–16 days.

Distribution. Widely distributed and common locally in much of Britain including Wales and Scotland, but absent from many areas which appear suitable.

Habitat. Woodland glades and ridings, wooded hillsides and wasteland bordering woods; also marshland and moors in the north.

Habits. Rapid flight backwards and forwards close to the ground, fluttering and then gliding. Seldom strays far from its own colony in a wood.

Life history. *Eggs*: pale yellow, laid singly on the underside of violet leaves. *Caterpillar*: just under 1 in. Brown, freckled with tiny white spots and covered with numerous tiny bristles. Spends the winter hibernating in a curled leaf on the ground, near its food-plant. Pupates suspended from a pad of silk on the undersurface of a violet leaf. *Chrysalis*: brown, with a lilac tinge, marked with a network of brown and black lines. *Butterfly*: single brooded, sometimes a second one in fine summers; first on the wing in early June, second in August.

Plate 5

1 **Painted Lady**, *Vanessa cardui* (p. 66) ♂ (sexes similar) × ⅔
1a underside × ⅔

2 **Red Admiral**, *Vanessa atalanta* (p. 67) ♂ (sexes similar) × ⅔
2a underside × ⅔

3 **Marsh Fritillary**, *Euphydryas aurinia* (p. 63) ♂ (sexes similar)
3a underside ♂
3b ♀
3c ab. *praeclara*, an Irish form, ♀
3d ab. *virgata*, with banded forewings, ♀

4 **Glanville Fritillary**, *Melitaea cinxia* (p. 62) ♂ (sexes similar)
4a underside ♂
4b ♀

5 **Heath Fritillary**, *Mellicta athalia* (p. 59) ♂ (sexes similar)
5a underside ♂
5b ♀
5c ♀ underside aberration with excess of black.

Scale: All life size except where otherwise indicated.

The Fritillaries on this plate, the Marsh, the Glanville and the Heath, have something in common; they all spend the winter as caterpillars, hibernating when quite small, in a 'nest' of silken threads on the ground, spun between the leaves of their food-plants. The Glanville is very local and its main headquarters is on the Isle of Wight, but the Marsh is widely distributed, and is found not only in marshland but in woodland ridings and even on grassy hillsides. The Glanville seldom varies, but the Marsh is noted for its many local county forms (figs. 3c and 3d). The Heath Fritillary, despite its name, is only found in wooded country, and is extremely local, being confined to a few southern counties, mainly in Kent and Essex and in Devon in the west; fig. 5c shows a good underside variety. Both the Painted Lady and the Red Admiral are migrants, which come to us most years in early summer from North Africa, and so may occur anywhere in the British Isles.

Plate 6

1 **Large Tortoiseshell**, *Nymphalis polychloros* (p. 69) ♀ (sexes similar, females always slightly larger than the males)
1*a* underside ♀

2 **Peacock**, *Inachis io* (p. 70) ♀ (sexes similar, females larger than males)
2*a* underside ♀
2*b* ab. *exoculata* Weym

3 **Camberwell Beauty**, *Nymphalis antiopa* (p. 71) ♂ (sexes similar, females slightly larger than males)
3*a* underside ♂

4 **Small Tortoiseshell**, *Aglais urticae* (p. 68) ♀ (sexes similar, females slightly larger than males)
4*a* underside ♀
4*b* ab. *bellieri* Cabeau
4*c* ab. *seminigra* Frowhawk

Scale: All butterflies on this plate are $\frac{2}{3}$ life size.

The Large Tortoiseshell has declined drastically in numbers in recent years, and it is now impossible to name a single locality in Britain where it can be found. It apparently disappeared from its former stronghold in Suffolk some years ago, and today only odd examples occasionally appear in wide-apart areas. We can only hope that this fine species might eventually recover a measure of its lost status. The Peacock and the Small Tortoiseshell are so widely distributed as to need no comment and both tend to throw aberrations, especially the latter which varies in ground colour from paper white, through yellow and gold to almost black in extreme varieties (figs. 4b and 4c). Fig. 2b shows a good variety of the Peacock. The Camberwell Beauty is now generally classed as an occasional vagrant, and most of the specimens probably reach this country travelling as 'stowaways' in the holds of timber ships from Scandinavia.

PEARL-BORDERED FRITILLARY

Clossiana euphrosyne **Pl. 4**

Description. Wing-span: $1\frac{1}{2}$ in. Sexes very similar. Ground colour rich golden-brown with a symmetrical pattern of black marks and dots on fore- and hind-wings; female often a little paler but more heavily marked. Underside markings similar on the fore-wings except for the tip which is blotched with rust-red and decorated with a row of seven silver lunules forming a chain round the outer margin. Colour forms and varieties are not uncommon. Plate 4: fig. 4c, ab. *nigricans*, approaching a melanic specimen.

Length of life. 14–16 days.

Distribution. Commonest in south and south-west England, but also in Wales, in Scotland as far north as Inverness and in parts of western Ireland.

Habitat. In woods and coppices where there are open clearings and ridings and dog violets grow in profusion.

Habits. Rapid fluttering flight close to the ground, often gliding for short distances. Will bask with wings spread, but rests with wings closed.

Life history. *Eggs:* yellowish-white, laid singly on the leaves of dog violet. *Caterpillar:* 1 in. Black on the back, greyish underneath and speckled with faint grey dots. Six rows of short black spines run down the body and on either side there is a broad chequered stripe of black and white just along the spiracles. Overwinters as a half-grown hibernating larva, hiding away near its food-plant in a dry curled leaf. Begins to feed again about the end of March. Pupates early in May. *Chrysalis:* pinkish-grey marked with fine brown lines and with rust-red raised points on the back. *Butterfly:* emerges at the end of May and on the wing for the first three weeks in June.

QUEEN OF SPAIN FRITILLARY   *Issoria lathonia*   **Pl. 3**

Description.   Wing-span: male 1¾ in., female 2 in. Sexes similar. Ground colour golden-brown with a pattern of black squares and blotches on all four wings and a double row of black spots running round the margins. Underside of fore-wings much lighter, the pattern of spotting repeated except for the tip which has silver marks; hind-wings heavily studded with silver discs and a chain of red-ringed silver spots on a yellowish background.

Length of life.   16–21 days.

Distribution.   A rare visitor to Britain. The few that reach our shores are usually found in the south and south-west of England. Breeds here occasionally, but never established.

Habitat.   Fields and meadows, any uncultivated land where wild flowers grow.

Habits.   Fast fluttering flight, alighting on the bare ground at frequent intervals to rest with wings spread wide. Feeds from flowers with wings closed.

Life history.   *Eggs*: pale yellow, laid singly on the leaves of wild pansy. *Caterpillar*: 1¼ in. Black, with two white lines running down the back; dotted with numerous white warts and rather bristly. Spends winter in hibernation. Pupates hanging head downwards, suspended from the tail end by hooks in a silk pad attached to the stem of its food-plant. *Chrysalis*: dark brown, dotted with various black and white marks and two rows of glistening metallic spots. *Butterfly*: double brooded on the Continent, on the wing in May and again in August and September. The odd vagrants seen here are nearly always second brood insects.

DARK GREEN FRITILLARY *Mesoacidalia aglaja* Pl. 4

Description. Wing-span: male $2\frac{1}{4}$ in., female $2\frac{1}{2}$ in. Sexes differ slightly. Male rich golden-brown with an intricate pattern of black lines, spots and markings on both fore- and hind-wings; the row of black triangular marks round the edge of the wings are well pronounced in this species. The female is a rather larger insect with spots and markings all slightly bigger than in the male. Underside colour and markings similar in both sexes; the chief characteristics are the green tints, shot with olive and gold, and the regular pattern of silver discs and spots forming a chain round the edge of the wing.
Length of life. 16–21 days.
Distribution. Our most widely distributed fritillary. Its range includes much of Britain and scattered parts of Ireland, but it has become scarcer in many areas in recent years.
Habitat. Downs and hillsides, occasionally in rough uncultivated pastures.
Habits. Powerful flight, effortlessly sweeping up and down hillsides. Males may be seen quartering over the short grass, searching for freshly emerged females.
Life history. *Eggs*: yellow, laid singly on the leaves of dog violet. *Caterpillar*: $1\frac{1}{2}$ in. Black and spiny with a row of reddish-orange spots low down on either side of the body. Overwinters as a minute hibernating caterpillar after eating its egg shell. Does not begin to feed again until the following April. Pupates in a 'tent' of violet leaves drawn together by silk threads, hanging head downwards and attached by the hind claspers to a pad of silk. *Chrysalis*: dark brown, with tawny-brown shading. *Butterfly*: single brooded; begins to emerge in late July and on the wing in August and even into September.

HIGH BROWN FRITILLARY *Fabriciana adippe* Pl. 4

Description. Wing-span: male $2\frac{1}{4}$ in., female $2\frac{1}{2}$ in. Sexes differ slightly. Male clear golden-brown with a pattern of black markings similar to those of the Dark Green Fritillary, except that they are rather more boldly defined, and on the lower edge of the fore-wings there is a patch of black scent scales. The female has a similar pattern, but is a slightly larger butterfly and the ground colour is a richer golden-brown. Underside is spangled with silver spots and discs outlined with black and has a scalloped marginal band edged with tawny crescents; the female has more silver marks than the male.

Length of life. 16–21 days.

Distribution. The scarcest of our larger fritillaries. Its range extends from southern England to the Lake District, but it has disappeared from a number of localities. Not found in Scotland or Ireland, and only sparingly in Wales.

Habitat. Woodland rides and clearings, especially attracted to flowering thistles.

Habits. Swift powerful flight, settling with wings spread wide on thistles or bramble blossom to feed on nectar; likes to roost in trees for the night and during dull sunless weather.

Life history. *Eggs*: yellow, laid singly on the leaves or stems of dog violet. Overwinters in this stage, hatching in mid- to late March. *Caterpillar*: $1\frac{1}{2}$ in. Light brown marked with two black and white lines along the back, and decorated with pink barbed spines. *Chrysalis*: light brown with dark brown mottling; studded with a double row of brilliant, silver-gilt metallic points down the length of its shell. Hangs suspended by the anal hooks fixed in a pad of silk attached to the underside of a leaf of its food-plant. *Butterfly*: emerges in mid-July and on the wing for most of August.

SILVER-WASHED FRITILLARY   *Argynnis paphia*

Pl. 4

Description.   Wing-span: 2½ in. Sexes differ. Male: bright orange-brown patterned with black spots on fore- and hind-wings; fore-wings carry triple black bars of scent scales. Female: tawny-olive ground colour deepening to greenish-olive at the base of the wings; black markings similar to the male but rather larger and scent scales lacking. Underside of fore-wings yellowish with a green tip and the black spotting of the upperside repeated in bold pattern; hind-wings shining bronze-green crossed by four bands of wavy, silvery scales; the outer edge silver, tinged with faint purple. Plate 4: fig. 3c, ab. *valesina*, a colour form of the female, only found in certain localities and always uncommon.

Length of life.   16–21 days.

Distribution.   Found mainly in southern and south-west England, but extending to Huntingdonshire and parts of Wales. Not in Scotland; widespread but local in Ireland.

Habitat.   Usually a woodland butterfly, but may be seen in flowery lanes in the West Country.

Habits.   Powerful fluttering and gliding flight along woodland ridings and in open glades; congregates in tangles of bramble blossom on which they feed with wings open. Females may be seen in woodlands searching for suitable tree-trunks on which to lay their eggs.

Life history.   *Eggs*: yellow, laid in the chinks of bark on old tree-trunks.   *Caterpillar*: 1½ in. Rich brown with two dull yellow stripes divided by a thin black line running down the back. Body covered with slender branching brown spines, the first pair protruding over the head like a pair of horns. Hibernates from August until March in a crevice near its partially eaten egg-shell. It takes no other food until it climbs down the tree-trunk and finds a dog violet plant the following spring. Pupates in June.   *Chrysalis*: light buff with two short pointed horns on the head; studded with five pairs of metallic points which glitter in the sun like gold. Attached by a silk pad to the underside of a violet leaf, hanging head downwards.   *Butterfly*: emerges in mid-July.

Description. Wing-span: $1\frac{1}{2}$ in. Sexes similar. Male ground colour rich orange-brown marked with a pattern that forms three transverse bands across the fore-wings; hind-wings similarly marked. All wings surrounded by black, edged with orange crescents. Female has lighter markings, more tawny-brown, and is a slightly larger butterfly. Underside fore-wings tawny-orange with the tip and border creamy-yellow, hind-wings ground colour deep cream, with a row of large orange crescent-shaped spots near the margin, followed by a conspicuous black wavy line and a concentration of orange streaks near the body. Plate 5: fig. 5c, rare underside variety, with a great excess of black scaling on the hind-wings, and heavily streaked fore-wings.

Length of life. 14–18 days.

Distribution. Very local and commonest in a restricted part of east Kent. Also in smaller numbers in Essex, Devon and Cornwall. Has been introduced into some localities in these counties.

Habitat. Strictly a woodland insect, breeding in areas recently cleared of undergrowth where its food-plant can thrive.

Habits. On emerging the butterflies tend to congregate in the open spaces of the woods; easy to find in late evening when they have gone to rest on grass stems, flower-heads or rushes. Weak, fluttery flight.

Life history. *Eggs*: yellowish-white, laid in quite large batches on the underside of leaves of cow-wheat. *Caterpillar*: 1 in. Gregarious. When fully grown gives the appearance of being nearly black although the under-surface is olive and the legs pale green. The body is covered with a mass of white tubercles and white spots from which stiff black hairs sprout. Spends the winter hibernating in a communal web at the base of the plant. *Chrysalis*: pale pearly-white, speckled with orange dots and streaked with black; hangs suspended by its anal hooks in a silken pad. *Butterfly*: first starts emerging in late June and on the wing for most of July.

Plate 7

1 **Purple Emperor**, *Apatura iris* (p. 73) ♂ (sexes quite distinct) × ⅔
1a underside ♂ × ⅔
1b ♀ × ⅔
1c ♂ variety with white bands partially missing. × ⅔ ab. *semi-iole* Frohawk

2 **White Admiral**, *Limenitis camilla* (p. 74) ♀ (sexes similar)
2a underside ♂
2b ♂
2c ♂ ab. *nigrina* Weym
2d ♂ ab. *obliterae* Robs. & Gard.

3 **Comma**, *Polygonia c-album* (p. 72) ♂ (sexes rather similar)
3a underside ♂
3b summer form, ♀, ab. *hutchinsoni* Robson
3c summer form ♂ underside, ab. *hutchinsoni* Robson

Scale: All the butterflies on this plate are life size except where indicated.

Both the Purple Emperor and the White Admiral are woodland species, and hibernate in the caterpillar stage when quite small; the former is far more local and can only be found in about six Midland and southern counties. Variation in both species consists of the absence, or partial absence, of the white bands on their wings (figs. 1c, 2c and 2d). The Comma passes the winter as a live butterfly in hibernation and appears on the wing again in early April. The first brood of butterflies emerges in July and are often of the light form known as variety *Hutchinsoni* (figs. 3b and 3c); these mate and produce a second brood in September, which soon retire into hibernation. Aberrations are uncommon, but specimens are sometimes caught with a ground colour of pale straw or deep chocolate, and occasionally the markings are joined up and heavily suffused with black scaling.

Plate 8

1 **Duke of Burgundy Fritillary,** *Hamearis lucina* (p. 75) ♂ (sexes rather similar)
1*a* underside ♂
1*b* ♀

2 **Long-tailed Blue,** *Lampides boeticus* (p. 76) ♂ (sexes quite distinct)
2*a* underside ♂
2*b* ♀

3 **Short-tailed Blue,** *Everes argiades* (p. 78) ♂ (sexes quite distinct)
3*a* underside ♂
3*b* ♀

4 **Small Blue,** *Cupido minimus* (p. 77) ♂ (sexes different)
4*a* underside ♂
4*b* ♀

5 **Silver-studded Blue,** *Plebejus argus* (p. 79) ♂ (sexes quite distinct)
5*a* underside ♂
5*b* underside ♂, ab. *flavescens* Tutt
5*c* ♀

6 **Adonis Blue,** *Lysandra bellargus* (p. 85, Pl. 9), ♂ underside ab. *tihhys* Esper
6*a* ♀ *gynandrous* specimen
6*b* ♀ ab. *striata* Tutt

7 **Chalk-hill Blue,** *Lysandra coridon* (p. 84, Pl. 9) ♂ underside ab. *bi-i-nigrum* Bright & Leeds
7*a* underside ♂, ab. *cinnus-obsoleta* Tutt

Scale: All the butterflies on this plate are life size.

The Duke of Burgundy is only a Fritillary in appearance and does not belong to this family at all; it is the only representative in Europe of the family Riodinidae, which is principally a South American group of butterflies. It passes the winter in the chrysalis stage. The Long and Short-tailed Blues are both rare migrant species and when they occur will most likely be met with in coastal areas in the south or south-west of England. The Small Blue is unlike any other member of this family as it hibernates as a fully grown caterpillar in the flower-head of its food-plant, kidney vetch, emerging in June. The Silver-studded Blue is on the wing a month later and has a wider distribution. The other figures on this plate show varieties of the Adonis and Chalk-hill Blues, including a *gynandrous* Adonis female streaked with male blue coloration and a very extreme underside Adonis with the spots elongated into black bars (fig. 6b).

Description. Wing-span: 1½ in. Sexes similar. Ground colour rich tawny-brown, banded and spotted with black in a variegated pattern; the black lines on the fore-wings form three transverse bands across the wings, more widely spaced in the female than in the male, and there is a marginal band of black spots. The hind-wing is broken up by two bands, the inner one tawny with black spots, and the outer one black with tawny spots. Underside fore-wings light tawny with few markings except for a creamy-yellow tip, hind-wings carry a wide white band, outlined in black across the centre of the wing followed by a tawny band enclosing a series of brown dots; the outer margin is pale cream.

Length of life. 14–16 days.

Distribution. Now confined to the Isle of Wight where it is locally common, though less so than formerly. Was introduced into the New Forest area, but has died out there.

Habitat. Mainly on the cliff slopes on the southern side of the Island, but isolated colonies occur in fields inland.

Habits. Does not take readily to the wing, preferring to sit basking with the wings wide open; feeble fluttering flight close to the ground. Sleeps on a grass stem with wings closed.

Life history. *Eggs*: yellow, laid in batches on the under-surface of narrow-leaved plantain. *Caterpillar*: 1 in. Gregarious. Black, speckled with white dots and covered with short, bristly black hair; head and feet red. Passes the winter as one of a large colony, hibernating in a silken web or 'tent' constructed at the base of the plant soon after hatching, and added to as required. Awakens in March and feeds voraciously on plantain leaves. *Chrysalis*: grey, mottled with dark brown and black, with curious raised yellow points. *Butterfly*: emerges in late May and on the wing during June.

Description. Wing-span: 1½ in. Sexes similar, but female larger. Ground colour varies enormously, from brick-red through tawny-red to yellowish-brown, according to the locality where it breeds. All forms carry a well-marked pale transverse band, wider in the female than the male. There is a broad coloured band round all four margins containing a series of yellow spots on the fore-wings, and black dots on the hind-wings; the areas close to the body are smoky-grey to black. Underside ground colour rust-brown with a well-defined marginal band containing a chain of black dots ringed with cream, an inner band of deep cream, and various cream blotches near the body. Plate 5: fig. 3c, ab. *praeclara*, a form found in Ireland; fig. 3d, banded fore-wing form, ab. *virgata*, not uncommon.

Length of life. 12–16 days.

Distribution. Locally in southern and especially south-west England, northward to parts of Wales and the Lake District. In a few areas in western Scotland, and common in some parts of Ireland.

Habitat. Not confined only to marshland, but also found in damp woodland rides and clearings, and on dry hillsides where its food-plant grows.

Habits. Lethargic flight, especially the female, which prefers to rest on the grass with wings expanded, but with the fore-wings drooped over the hind-wings. Males more active, but seldom fly more than a few yards at a time.

Life history. *Eggs*: bright yellow at first, becoming darker and then greyish-brown just before hatching. Laid in untidy heaps on the under-surface of the leaves of devil's-bit scabious. *Caterpillar*: just over 1 in. Gregarious, living in a silken web spun low down between the leaves of the food-plant, and coming out to feed in sunny weather. Black and bristly, with a line of white dots low down on either side of the body. Overwinters in a large hibernating colony, hidden away in a silken web often just underground at the base of the plant. *Chrysalis*: hangs suspended from a leaf, attached to a pad of silk by hooks at the tail end. Greyish-white, boldly spotted with black and orange dots. *Butterfly*: emerges towards the end of May, and on the wing for most of June.

Plate 9

1 **Brown Argus,** *Aricia agestis* (p. 82) ♂ (sexes very similar)
1a underside ♂
1b ♀

2 **Brown Argus** ♂, subsp. *salmacis* (p. 82)
2a underside ♂ subsp. *salmacis*
2b ♀ subsp. *salmacis*

3 **Brown Argus** ♂ subsp. *artaxerxes* (p. 82)
3a underside ♂ subsp. *artaxerxes*
3b ♀ subsp. *artaxerxes*

4 **Common Blue,** *Polyommatus icarus* (p. 83) ♂ (sexes differ)
4a underside ♂
4b ♀
4c ♀ ab. *supracaerulea* Oberthur (Irish form)

5 **Chalk-hill Blue,** *Lysandra coridon* (p. 84, Pl. 8) ♂
5a underside ♂
5b ♀
5c ♀ ab. *semi-syngrapha* Tutt
5d ♂ ab. *marginata* Tutt
5e ♂ ab. *fowleri* South

6 **Adonis Blue,** *Lysandra bellargus* (p. 85, Pl. 8) ♂ (sexes differ)
6a underside ♂
6b ♀
6c Halved *gynandromorph*

Scale: All butterflies on this plate are life size.

The Brown Argus and its two subspecies var. *salmacis* from the Midlands and var. *artaxerxes* from Scotland, are chosen to show good examples of these forms, but there are of course many intermediates. The Common Blue is double brooded over much of the British Isles, except northern Scotland and parts of Ireland, and can be seen on the wing in early and late summer (fig. 4c shows a blue Irish female form). The Chalk-hill Blue is a single brooded butterfly which emerges in late July and may still be on the wing early in September. The Adonis Blue is a double brooded species, emerging in late May and June, while the second brood flies during the latter part of August and into early October. The members of this family are noted for variation of colour forms, sexual aberrations and variation in the spotting on the underside. Fig. 6c shows a very rare Adonis halved gynandromorph, while fig. 5c is an example of ab. *semi-syngrapha* found in the Chalk-hill Blue, while figs. 5d and 5e are male aberrations.

Plate 10

1 **Large Copper,** *Lycaena dispar rutilus* ♂ (sexes differ)
1a underside ♂
1b ♀

2 **Small Copper,** *Lycaena phlaeas* (p. 89) ♂ (sexes similar)
2a underside ♂
2b ♀
2c ♀ ab. *caeruleopunctata* Ruhl
2d ♂ ab. *fasciata* Strecker
2e ♂ ab. *fuscata* Tutt
2f ♂ ab. *bipunctata* Tutt
2g ♂ ab. *schmidtii* Gerhardt
2h ♂ showing *homoeosis*

3 **Large Blue,** *Maculinea arion* (p. 87) ♂ (sexes differ slightly)
3a underside ♂
3b ♀
3c ♀ ab. *insubrica* Vorbr.
3d ♂ underside ab. *subtus-impunctata* Oberthur
3e ♂ ab. *alconides* Aur.

4 **Holly Blue,** *Celastrina argiolus* (p. 88) ♂ (sexes differ)
4a underside ♂
4b ♀ spring form
4c ♀ summer form

Scale: All butterflies on this plate are life size.

The indigenous Large Copper became extinct in Britain during the 1840s but a Dutch race, *Lycaena dispar batava* (p. 90), has been introduced here, and is established because of strict protection, in Wood Walton Fen, Huntingdonshire. The closely related Continental form *L. dispar rutilus* is illustrated here, and very closely resembles the other two species.

The Small Copper is one of our most widespread small butterflies, and is almost continuously brooded from April to October. It is subject to much variation in ground colour and changes in the spotting on the fore-wings (figs 2c, 2d, 2e, 2f and 2g). Many of the forms have been named. Fig. 2h shows a very rare form known as *homoeosis* in which the pattern and structure of the wing is transposed to another part of the wing. This curious freak of nature is known to have a genetic basis and occurs also in other insects, in fish and in animals including humans. The Large Blue is now one of our rarest butterflies and is included in the protected list. It comes out in late June and July, and is found in a very restricted part of north Devon, and possibly, though by no means certainly, in north Cornwall and the Cotswold Hills. It is on the verge of extinction and if found should on no account be taken. In the Holly Blue there is a marked difference between the spring and summer forms of the female (figs. 4b and 4c), otherwise variation is rare.

PAINTED LADY *Vanessa cardui* Pl. 5

Description. Wing-span: 2¼ in. Sexes similar. Ground colour brownish-pink decorated with a dark brown irregular band across the forewings; the whole of the tips are black except for seven well-defined square spots. Hind-wings have a chain of five round black spots running parallel to the outer margin, except that the tip is ochreous, while the hind-wings are washed entirely with this yellowish tint, mottled with greenish-brown, and marked with a row of quite large blue-centred eye-spots.

Length of life. 21–30 days.

Distribution. This attractive immigrant varies considerably in numbers from year to year. Common and widespread in some seasons, scarce in others. It often breeds here, but never becomes established.

Habitat. Fields of flowering lucerne or clover, cultivated flowers in parks and gardens, meadows and downland.

Habits. Rapid powerful flight which can be sustained over long distances. On reaching a desired destination will patrol a stretch of ground, backwards and forwards for days on end, performing an elaborate courtship display. Feeds and sleeps with wings closed; often basks in sun on bare ground with wings open wide.

Life history. *Eggs*: pale green, laid singly on the upper surface of thistle leaves. *Caterpillar*: just over 1 in. Black and spiny along the back, divisions between the segments grey; a broken yellow stripe runs down the length of the body from the fourth segment. Feeds on the under-surface of the leaves, avoiding the main rib and sharper spines. *Chrysalis*: pale pinkish-grey, often tinted with gold and copper, and striped and dotted with black markings. It hangs suspended by hooks from a pad of silk spun round a stem or twig. *Butterfly*: no resting period. In its native haunts, the coastal districts of North Africa, it is continuously brooded and early in the year the first waves of migrants cross the Mediterranean and colonize the South of France. As brood succeeds brood they spread all over Europe and by May or June some have usually crossed the Channel and begun breeding in this country.

RED ADMIRAL   *Vanessa atalanta*   Pl. 5

Description.   Wing-span: 2½ in. Sexes similar. Ground colour velvety-black with wide scarlet bands across the fore-wings, and tips decorated with white blotches and spots; hind-wings edged with a wide scarlet band marked with black spots. Underside markings a complicated pattern in grey, brown and buff with a few bluish spots round the margin.

Length of life.   21–30 days.

Distribution.   Another immigrant that varies in numbers from year to year. Sometimes very common in gardens in late summer. Breeds here, but not established.

Habitat.   In private gardens and municipal parks; in the country-side round nettle-beds and waste-ground where wild flowers grow in profusion.

Habits.   Strong powerful flight, roosting at night in trees. Once having found a territory to its liking, the butterfly usually haunts the vicinity and returns day after day to the same place to feed from cultivated or wild flowers. Attracted to buddleia, valerian, rotting fruit and sap exuding from damaged trees; feed with wings partially open or closed.

Life history.   *Eggs*: green, laid singly on the edge of stinging nettle leaves. *Caterpillar*: 1¾ in. Several colour forms, may be black, grey, or greenish-grey and very spiny; an irregular wavy stripe in yellow or white runs along the side of the body. Feeds hidden from view in a folded leaf sewn together by strands of silk. *Chrysalis*: reddish-grey with powdery bloom, studded with metallic gold spots; hangs suspended in a kind of 'tent' of nettle leaves spun together by the larva just before it pupates. *Butterfly*: continuously brooded in southern Europe. When over-crowding occurs or the herbage along the Mediterranean shrivels up in the summer heat, the butterflies migrate north to breed, and in most years some reach the shores of Britain. Most of the Red Admirals bred in this country make their way south when autumn approaches.

SMALL TORTOISESHELL *Aglais urticae* Pl. 6

Description. Wing-span: 2 in. Ground colour tawny-orange with a chain of violet-blue spots encircling all four wings near the outer edges. Three well-defined square black marks divided by two smaller yellow ones run along the front edge of the fore-wings, terminating in a white blotch; two small black spots and a larger blotch of black and of yellow near the centre complete the normal pattern of the fore-wings. On the hind-wings there is a large expanse of black next to the body. In contrast the underside markings are dull and drab, dark brown near the body with a wide ochreous band spreading towards the outer margins. Plate 6: fig. 4c, a rare form, has the black spots on the fore-wings joined in a continuous band, the two side spots missing, and the hind-wings are much darker than normal. Numerous colour forms occur, fig. 4b shows a specimen with pale cream ground colouring.

Length of life. Summer brood 3–4 weeks, autumn brood 9–10 months.

Distribution. Our commonest brightly coloured butterfly. Found almost everywhere in Britain and Ireland.

Habitat. Parks and gardens, and throughout the countryside generally.

Habits. Wild erratic flight, the butterflies much given to chasing each other low over the ground, in wide sweeps over fields and meadows and along country lanes. Feeds with wings open or half open, rests with them closed.

Life history. *Eggs*: pale green, laid in a large batch on the underside of stinging nettle leaves. *Caterpillar*: just under 1 in. Dark greyish-green at first, becoming darker with distinct yellow lines down each side of the body and covered with short, yellowish, black-tipped spines. Gregarious, living in silken nests among nettle leaves until half-grown, and then splitting up to feed singly or in small groups of two or three in folded nettle leaves. *Chrysalis*: dull brown, occasionally a lighter shade washed with a golden sheen. Always suspended from a stem or twig, hanging head downwards. *Butterfly*: overwinters in hibernation, usually inside a building, from October until the following March. First brood emerge in June, the second brood in August.

Description.   Wing-span: male 2¼ in., female 2½ in. Sexes similar. The ground colour is a rich tawny-brown shaded with ochreous yellow. Forewings carry two large rectangular marks and a double spot on the front margin; there are also four smaller black marks in a regular pattern together with flecks of yellow. The hind-wings are boldly marked with a large black blotch midway along the front edge. The edges of all four wings are scalloped and round the margins there is a wavy black band and a chain of crescent-shaped violet spots running parallel to it, only faintly discernible in some specimens, more bold in others. The female is always a rather larger insect. Undersides covered with thin black bristles, particularly thick round the body; wings are banded on the outer half in yellowish-brown with dark brown at the base; outer margins edged with an irregular purplish-grey band.

Length of life.   9–9½ months.

Distribution.   Fairly widely distributed in England early this century, but now a rarity. Its last stronghold was near Ipswich, but it seems to have died out there. Odd examples are sometimes reported from different parts of the country.

Habitat.   Flies along elm-bordered lanes and fields, in woods and forests, preferring the outskirts to the interior.

Habits.   Strong fluttering and soaring flight. Is fond of basking on the bare earth, on sunny pathways in a wood, with wings spread wide, and will fly up at the slightest disturbance.

Life history.   *Eggs*: yellow, laid in early May in bracelets on the terminal shoots of common elm, wych elm, and less frequently on sallow or willow, aspen, birch and white beam.   *Caterpillar*: 1⅝ in. Gregarious, living together in an untidy silken web spun between twiglets. Ground colour black, covered with white hairy warts and sharp yellow branching spines. There are two yellow lines down the back divided by a thin black one, and the sides are marked with amber and under-surface with purplish-grey. Pupates away from the tree, hanging head downwards from any convenient ledge or twig, attached to a silk pad by its hind-claspers.   *Chrysalis*: colour varies from dull brown to dark grey, very spiny, with a double row of raised points outlined with silver-gilt discs.   *Butterfly*: hibernates from August to April, usually hiding away in piles of brushwood or dense thickets of undergrowth; has been known to pass the winter in a hollow tree or hole in a bank. May appear in March if weather favourable.

Description. Wing-span: $2\frac{1}{4}$ in. Sexes identical. Ground colour rich wine-red. On the front edge of the fore-wings are two black marks separated by a suffused yellow area, and a conspicuous eye-spot occupies the whole of the wing-tip. The centre of the eye is black and wine-red with a crescent of amethyst on the outer edge, marked with several white dots. Below the eye are two small bright blue spots. The hind-wings also carry large eye-spots of gleaming blue with black centres encircled with an ashy-grey band. The margins of all the wings are heavily scalloped. Underside very dark purplish-brown, marked with a mass of fine lines; males are rather darker than the females. Plate 6: fig. 2b, ab. *exoculata*, a rare variety with 'blind' eye-spots on the hind-wings.

Length of life. $10-10\frac{1}{2}$ months.

Distribution. Well distributed in Britain as far north as mid-Scotland, and often common in southern England though numbers differ from year to year. Widespread in Ireland.

Habitat. Private gardens and parks, generally in the countryside where nettle-beds are established.

Habits. Fast fluttering and gliding flight low over the ground. Likes to bask on the bare earth in the sun with wings pressed flat on the soil. Males appear to play games and perform wild aerobatics in the air for hours on end.

Life history. *Eggs*: green, laid in May in large untidy batches on the under-surface of stinging nettle leaves. *Caterpillar*: $1\frac{3}{4}$ in. Gregarious, living in a thick white silken tent-like web among nettle stems. Glossy black, covered with rows of shining black spines and dotted with white warts from which sprout fine hairs. *Chrysalis*: colour varies from greenish-yellow to dull brown, usually found away from the nettle-bed as the caterpillars wander away to pupate, suspending themselves, head downwards, from a twig in a hedgerow. The pupa has two sharp horns on the head and a double row of sharp points along the abdomen. *Butterfly*: hibernates from October to March, but if disturbed will make a rustling noise by rotating the hind-wings. This has been likened to the hiss of a snake. Often comes into houses to spend the winter, and in the countryside shelters in hollow trees, in evergreen bushes or down rabbit holes.

CAMBERWELL BEAUTY *Nymphalis antiopa*

Pl. 6

Description. Wing-span: male $2\frac{1}{2}$ in., female 3 in. Sexes similar, female always larger than the male. Ground colour dark purplish-brown and wings scalloped, edged with a pale yellow band dusted with brown scaling. Two triangular yellow marks at the front edge of the fore-wings, and a row of violet-blue spots on a black band inside the yellow margin of each wing. The underside is black with a mass of short spiny hairs near the body; the marginal band appears almost white.

Length of life. $9\frac{1}{2}$–10 months.

Distribution. A rare immigrant from northern Europe, seen more often in eastern England. Does not breed here in the wild state, but some examples recorded might be from foreign stock, bred in captivity in this country, and liberated.

Habitat. Woods and forest where there are birch groves or fir plantations which resemble their natural habitat in Scandinavia.

Habits. Powerful gliding and fluttering flight, often soaring high up over the tree-tops. Will feed on sallow blossom in the spring, but prefers to suck up sap exuding from damaged trees or rotting fruit in autumn. Basks in the sun with wings spread wide, on the ground or on tree-trunks.

Life history. *Eggs*: golden-brown, deepening to purple and finally dark grey; laid in a bracelet round the terminal shoots of sallow or willow bushes. *Caterpillar*: just over 2 in. Gregarious, for the whole life, feeding together at the tips of twigs and moving backwards in a cluster, as the foliage is consumed, to a thick silken web in the fork of a branch where they shelter at night. Covered with long sharp black spines, the body velvety-black, sprouting white hairs at the base of each spine. Along the back is a row of conspicuous dark-red marks, and the feet are also the same colour. Wanders some distance from the tree and hangs head downwards to pupate, suspended by its hind-claspers from a silk pad. *Chrysalis*: light buff-coloured, covered with a pinkish-grey powdery substance, like the 'bloom' on a grape; at the head end there are two projections like a beak and there is a row of sharp spines on the body. *Butterfly*: overwinters in caves, thickets of wood, stacked pit-props or felled timber. Not a resident species of this country, but believed to reach Britain as a migrant or as an involuntary stowaway on timber ships from Scandinavia, usually being seen during the autumn months.

Description. Wing-span: $1\frac{3}{4}$ in. Sexes differ slightly. Male is a rich reddish-brown, spotted with dark chocolate and black marks. On the front edge of the fore-wing there is a squarish black blotch and nearer the body three smaller round black spots and various other small dark marks; the inner margin is decorated with a row of buff spots. The hind-wings are similarly patterned. Female rather lighter in ground colour with the marginal band of buff spots more pronounced on the hind-wings. Sexual difference more distinct in the underside colour and markings, male being patterned in a marbled effect of brown, black, greenish and buff, while the female is plainer and more greyish-brown. Both sexes carry a clear white C-shaped mark in the centre of each hind-wing. In the summer brood a proportion of the females are much lighter; this form is known as ab. *hutchinsoni*.   Plate 7: fig. 3b, female upperside, summer form; fig 3c, male underside, summer form.

Length of life. $8-8\frac{1}{2}$ months; summer brood 14–20 days.

Distribution. Common locally in south and south-west England. Its range extends northwards to south Yorkshire where it is now less common than a few years ago. Not in Scotland or Ireland.

Habitat. Woodland glades and clearings, margins of woods and country lanes.

Habits. Rapid flight, settling frequently to bask with expanded wings on tree-trunks, leaves or on the bare ground. Seldom strays far from the home locality. Visits gardens to feed from flowering sallow and cherry blossom in spring, buddleia bushes in high summer, and the Michaelmas daisies in early autumn.

Life history. *Eggs*: green, laid singly during April and May at the edge of nettle leaves or on elm, wych elm, red currant, and hop. *Caterpillar*: $1\frac{3}{8}$ in. At the front end of the body, the back is yellow and from the sixth to the tenth segments white; the sides are dark brown streaked with grey markings. Seven rows of spines run the length of the body. It has the appearance of a bird dropping when resting in a curled position on the leaf. *Chrysalis*: hangs suspended from a leaf-stalk; pinkish-grey with dark olive-green markings sometimes of a metallic bronze sheen. There are two short horns on the head and a prominent hump just behind. Decorated with six burnished silver discs and a series of small yellow points. *Butterfly*: overwinters right out in the open on a tree-trunk or in the shelter of a branch; on the wing again in late March. Double brooded, first brood emerging in July, the second in August, and on the wing until the butterflies retire into hibernation late in October.

Description. Wing-span: male 2½ in., female 2¾ in. Sexes differ. Male ground colour bitter chocolate-brown shot with a brilliant purple sheen on both fore- and hind-wings. There is a broken white band on the fore-wings and a broad continuous one on the hind-wings, which are also decorated with a rust-red ring encircling a round black spot. Female has exactly similar markings but no iridescent purple on its wings. The margins of the wings are scalloped and just inside the dark edge runs a band of grey. Underside white markings are similar on the fore-wings, but the ground colour is a mixture of red-brown, buff and dark-brown, with the margins pearly-grey with a prominent blue-centred eye-spot. Hind-wings carry a wide wedge-shaped white streak across the centre, edged with rust-red, and a deep pearly-grey margin. Plate 7: fig. 1c, ab. *semi-iole*, a rare variety with fore-wing bands almost missing.

Length of life. 15–25 days.

Distribution. Uncommon but found locally in many wooded areas in southern England. Its range extends to Oxfordshire and Northamptonshire. Not in Scotland or Ireland.

Habitat. In large woodlands and forests, and private estates.

Habits. Likes to soar, with a powerful gliding flight, around the topmost branches of the highest trees, usually oak, in the vicinity. Females descend at midday to search for sallow bushes in the undergrowth on which to deposit their eggs. Both sexes are attracted to carrion, from which they suck juices.

Life history. *Eggs*: greenish-brown, laid singly on the upper surface of sallow leaves. *Caterpillar*: 1¾ in. Soft light green, speckled with white dots. Pointed at both ends, the head decorated with two greenish-blue horns knobbed with red, giving it a slug-like appearance. The body is marked with six oblique light yellow stripes along the sides. Hibernates over winter on a bed of silk in a fork of a branch or twig. Begins to feed in March and pupates beneath a leaf, after first securing the leaf stalk to the twig with silk, in late June or early July. *Chrysalis*: silver-green, exactly matching the under-surface of a sallow leaf. The head bears two pointed horns. *Butterfly:* emerges in July and on the wing during the first half of August.

WHITE ADMIRAL   *Limenitis camilla*   Pl. 7

Description.   Wing-span: $2\frac{1}{4}$ in. Sexes almost identical. Ground colour dark blackish-brown with a white band, broken by black veins, crossing both fore- and hind-wings. Black spots round the margins form a chain right round all four wings. Underside ground colour rusty-brown, with three rows of black spots set in the marginal band, the wide white bands on the upperside repeated on the underside. Between these white bands and the body there is an area of greyish-blue. The female is always a slightly larger insect and the ground colour is a little paler than in the male. Plate 7: fig. 2c, ab. *nigrina*, white bands missing; fig. 2d, ab. *obliterae*, bands indistinct, both forms uncommon.

Length of life.   14–18 days.

Distribution.   Mainly in wooded areas of southern England, but found more sparingly as far north as Lincoln. Less common in many places than formerly. Not in Scotland or Ireland.

Habitat.   Woods and forests, flying in clearings and along sunny ridings.

Habits.   Most graceful gliding and fluttering flight; alights with wings wide open on bramble blossom to feed on nectar.

Life history.   *Eggs*: olive-green, laid singly on the edges of honeysuckle leaves. *Caterpillar*: just over 1 in. Bright green speckled with white dots; a whitish line, edged with purple, runs low down along the legs. The second and third segments of the body are larger than the rest, giving the body a humped appearance. On five of these segments there are two long, branched spines of red-brown; shorter spines decorate the rest of the body. Hibernates inside a folded honeysuckle leaf, which is securely fixed to the stem by silk threads before the caterpillar retires for the winter. Begins to feed in late March or April. *Chrysalis*: most curious and irregular in shape. The head carries two ear-like points and on the body is a prominent keel, shaped like a hooked nose. The body is studded with brilliant silver-gilt spots, and hangs suspended from a twig head downwards, attached by anal hooks to a silken pad. *Butterfly*: on the wing from mid-July to mid-August.

DUKE OF BURGUNDY FRITILLARY

Hamearis lucina **Pl. 8**

Description. Wing-span: 1 in. Sexes very similar. Ground colour brownish-black, fore-wings marked with two irregular transverse bands of orange-brown streaks, hind-wings darker, with a few streaks of the same colour concentrated near the centre of the wings; margins surrounded by black spots enclosed in orange crescents. Female more heavily marked with lighter streaks and spots than the male. Main difference between the sexes is that the male has only two pairs of legs (the third pair being only rudimentary and undeveloped) while the female has the normal three pairs common to all butterflies. Underside pattern similar on the fore-wings but on a lighter ground colour, and the hind-wings carrying two rows of white dashes forming separate broken bands.

Length of life. 12–16 days.

Distribution. Locally in England only, and commonest in the southern counties, but also found in the Lake District and north-east Yorkshire. Less common than formerly in many places.

Habitat. On sunny hillsides and often in rough pastures bordering on woods.

Habits. Very local, taking only short fast flights over a limited area; settles on flowers with wings half open.

Life history. *Eggs*: yellowish-white, laid in small clusters on the under-surface of primrose or cowslip leaves. *Caterpillar*: ½ in. Buff-coloured, with a dark line down the back through which a black spot shows up on each segment. Thickly covered with soft white hair and clusters of bristles. *Chrysalis*: pale creamy-white, short and rounded and very bristly, dotted and flecked with black spots and streaks; attached to a leaf or stem by a silken thread round the waist. Over-winters among the rotting leaves at the base of the plant. *Butterfly*: emerges in May.

Description.   Wing-span: $1\frac{1}{4}$ in. Sexes differ. Male light purple with a narrow black border round the margins of all four wings. In the female the outer half of the fore-wings and the entire front edge are black, while the remainder of these wings are iridescent purple shot with bright blue; hind-wings brownish-black, powdered with blue at the base. Along the lower margin there is a row of black spots, ringed with white, and inside this is a band of wedge-shaped greyish marks. Underside markings similar in both sexes: buff with numerous transverse slightly wavy lines and dashes of brown, and a black eye-spot in the corner of the hind-wings, which is slightly elongated and ends in a tiny tail.

Length of life.   14–18 days.

Distribution.   An extremely rare visitor from Europe. In most years not a single example is recorded, but has bred occasionally in southern England.

Habitat.   Anywhere on the south coast, usually in late summer; the most likely place is a garden or park where the butterfly comes to feed on nectar.

Habits.   Fast flight, flickering around flowering trees and bushes and settling with closed wings to feed from flowers.

Life history.   *Eggs*: bluish-white, laid singly on the stem or at the base of a bud of any of their food-plants, including various vetches, bladder senna, Spanish broom and tree lupin. *Caterpillar*: $\frac{3}{4}$ in. Pea-green with a darker green line down the back, and three irregular broken wavy bands along the side; feeds by burrowing its head into the seed-pods and eating the developing seeds. Turns a dull pink and then pupates inside a curled leaf, drawing the opening together with strands of silk, and resting on a pad of silk with a girdle round the waist. *Chrysalis*: pinkish-cream, traced with fine dark lines and flecked with dark marks. Smooth and rounded at both ends. *Butterfly*: breeds continuously on the Continent.

SMALL BLUE   *Cupido minimus*   Pl. 8

Description.   Wing-span: $\frac{7}{8}$ in. Sexes differ. Male greyish-black dusted with light silvery-blue scales near the body. Female dark brown with no suggestion of blue. Underside markings similar in both sexes: a central black discoidal spot and a chain of seven white-ringed black dots running parallel to the margin; hind-wings dotted with scattered black spots, twelve in all.

Length of life.   10–14 days.

Distribution.   Distributed very locally, and commonest in southern England. Its range extends to Northumberland and a few parts of eastern Scotland. Also in western Ireland.

Habitat.   Grassy hillsides and downland; disused chalk-pits are favoured localities.

Habits.   Rapid fluttering flight, low over the ground, but only for short distances; settles for the night, often in small companies, on grass stems.

Life history.   *Eggs*: pale green, laid singly and tucked into the flower-heads of kidney vetch. *Caterpillar*: pale green or sometimes pale yellow, marked with pink streaks along the sides and a white line along the back. It burrows into the flower-heads to feed on the developing seeds, and is sometimes cannibalistic. Hibernates when fully grown, hiding away over winter in a hibernaculum of silk spun amongst the flowers of its food-plant. Pupates upright on a grass blade. *Chrysalis*: creamy-buff suffused with grey and marked with black blotches and spots; the surface is rough and covered with fine bristles. *Butterfly*: emerges at the end of May.

Description. Wing-span: 1⅛ in. Sexes differ. Male light violet, with a narrow black margin which is broken up into a short band of black spots on the hind-wing; there is a short tail about midway along the hind-margin of the lower wing. Female dull brown suffused with blue scaling on the basal half of all four wings; hind-wings carry two small orange spots near the tail. Underside very similar in both sexes: pale grey with a tinge of bluish-grey; fore-wings outlined with a chain of black spots and the hind-wings sprinkled with more black dots. Along the margin are a series of black marks, three of them edged with bright orange; the spot closest to the tail is surrounded with metallic silver.

Length of life. 10–14 days.

Distribution. Another very rare visitor from Europe. The few examples recorded in the last century were found in southern and south-west England.

Habitat. Coastal districts on waste-land where wild flowers grow; possibly in gardens or parks beside the sea in this country.

Habits. Quick fluttering flight, resting in the sun with wings open on flower-heads or grasses.

Life history. *Eggs*: greenish-white, laid singly on the leaves of bird's-foot trefoil. *Caterpillar*: ⅜ in. Light green, with a darker green stripe running down the back and oblique pale green stripes along the sides. Skin covered with short stiff hairs. Turns pinkish-buff and hibernates over winter in the dead curled leaves of its food-plant. Awakes in spring and pupates in an upright position on the food-plant, attached by a silken girdle and a pad at the tail end. *Chrysalis*: light green, peppered with black dots; a broken black streak along the back and a row of black spots along each side. *Butterfly*: double brooded in northern France, treble brooded in southern Europe, the butterflies on the wing in May, and then again in July and August.

Description.   Wing-span: 1 in. Sexes quite distinct. Male light violet-blue; both fore- and hind-wings have black outer margins with startlingly white fringes, the hind-wings decorated with a row of black spots. Female deep bronze-brown with the margins edged with spots, brown on the fore-wings and ringed with orange on the hind-wings; there is usually a slight dusting of violet scales near the body. Underside pattern the same in both sexes, in the male the ground colour greyish-blue, in the female pale coffee-coloured. A bold pattern of evenly distributed black spots covers both fore- and hind-wings. The marginal band on the fore-wings is a bold series of oval black spots ringed with white and edged with black, hind-wings edged with metallic silver-centred black spots, which run parallel to a deep orange band outlined with black crescent-shaped marks. Plate 8: fig. 5b, ab. *flavescens*, normal orange spots replaced by lemon yellow ones.

Length of life.   12–15 days.

Distribution.   Mainly in southern and south-west England, and less common than formerly. It seems to have disappeared from localities in Lincolnshire and Westmorland where it was once common. Local in Wales and Anglesey. Not in Scotland or Ireland. A small race is found in north Wales.

Habitat.   Two distinct types of country; open glades, in woods, on heaths and commons where heather grows, or on hillsides and downland where there is gorse and broom.

Habits.   Rather weak fluttering flight, settling frequently with wings open to bask in the sun; never strays more than a few hundred yards from its home ground.

Life history.   *Eggs*: white, laid singly on the stems of heather, gorse or broom. Overwinters in this stage, hatching in late March.   *Caterpillar*: ½ in. Pale green with a purple stripe along the back, edged with white lines; sides of body marked with a series of wavy darker green and purplish-brown lines, with a white band just above the legs. Rough skin covered with pale hairs. At first feeds on the opening flowers, later on the seeds. Pupates low down on the plant, securing itself with a few strands of silk round the body.   *Chrysalis*: pale yellowish-green with white wing-cases; smooth and rounded at the head.   *Butterfly*: emerges in late July.

Plate 11

1   **Purple Hairstreak**, *Quercusia quercus* (p. 93) ♂ (sexes distinct)
1*a* underside ♂
1*b* ♀

2   **Brown Hairstreak**, *Thecla betulae* (p. 92) ♂ (sexes differ)
2*a* underside ♂
2*b* ♀

3   **Black Hairstreak**, *Strymonidia pruni* (p. 95) ♂ (sexes differ slightly)
3*a* underside ♂
3*b* ♀

4   **White-letter Hairstreak**, *Strymonidia w-album* (p. 94) ♂ (sexes differ slightly)
4*a* underside ♀
4*b* underside ♂

5   **Green Hairstreak**, *Callophrys rubi* (p. 91) ♂ (sexes almost identical)
5*a* underside ♂
5*b* underside ab. *inferopunctata* Tutt

Scale: All butterflies on this plate are life size.

Hairstreak butterflies were given the title because of the fine, hair-like lines on the under-surface of the wings. The Green and Brown species are so named because of their underside coloration, and there can be some confusion between the Black and the White-letter species because, of the two, the latter is more truly black on the upper side. The Black Hairstreak is dusky brown, with orange lunules on the wing edges, especially in the female. All spend the winter in the egg stage, laid on twigs of their food-plant next to a bud, except the Green Hairstreak which overwinters in the chrysalis stage on the surface of the ground among dead leaves or other litter.

Plate 12

1 **Swallow-tail**, *Papilio machaon* (p. 98) ♀ (sexes similar) × ⅔
1*a* underside ♀ × ⅔
1*b* ♂ ab. *obscura* Frohawk × ⅔

2 **Large White**, *Pieris brassicae* (p. 100) ♂ (sexes differ) × ⅔
2*a* underside ♀ × ⅔
2*b* ♀ × ⅔

3 **Small White**, *Pieris rapae* (p. 101) ♂ (sexes differ)
3*a* underside ♂
3*b* ♀

4 **Green-veined White**, *Pieris napi* (p. 102) ♂ (sexes differ)
4*a* underside ♂
4*b* ♀
4*c* ♀ ab. *confluens* Schima (an Irish form)
4*d* ♂ ab. *sulphurea* Schoyen (originally an Irish form)
4*e* ♀ ab. *aurea* Mosley (Scottish)

Scale: All life size except where otherwise indicated.

The Swallow-tail is the only British representative of the large
family Papilionidae, which includes many more species known
throughout the world for their large size, brilliant colours, and in
many cases tailed hind-wings. It is our largest butterfly, and now
breeds only in the Norfolk Broads area, but in the last century it had
a wider distribution in this country. Examples of the Swallow-tail
occasionally seen elsewhere are more likely to be escapees from the
cages of butterfly breeders, or odd vagrants that have immigrated
from Europe where the species is common and has a wide range. Very
rarely melanic specimens appear in the Norfolk localities, and they are
highly prized by collectors. The Large White population in this
country is often reinforced by migrations from the Continent, and the
same may be said of the Small White, but usually not on such a large
scale. Both butterflies have two broods in the season, and in hot dry
summers there can be a partial third brood. The Green-veined White
is also double brooded, and there are distinct named forms in Scotland
(fig. 4e) and in Ireland (fig. 4c) where a very rare yellow form (fig.
4d) is also known to occur.

BROWN ARGUS *Aricia agestis* Pl. 9

Description. Wing-span: 1 in. Sexes differ slightly. Male is a dark rich brown, fringed with white and edged with a chain of orange-red spots on both fore- and hind-wings. In the female these spots are always larger and the fore-wings are slightly more rounded than in the male. Both sexes have a small black spot in the centre of the fore-wing. On the underside, the male is light greyish-brown, and the female pale brown, with seven white-ringed black spots on the fore-wing and twelve on the hind-wing. The wings are patterned with a band of orange spots along the margins, edged with black and white crescents. There are two distinct forms of the Brown Argus. The typical form *agestis* (Plate 9: figs. 1, 1a, 1b) is found in the south. The Scottish form, sub-species *artaxerxes* (figs. 3, 3a, 3b), has a round white spot in the middle of the fore-wing in both sexes and the spots on the underside are white or may have small black dots in the centre. The intermediate form is known as subspecies *salmacis*, or Castle Eden (figs. 2, 2a, 2b).

Length of life. 12–14 days.

Distribution. The *agestis* form is well distributed in southern England, but numbers fluctuate from year to year. The *salmacis* form occurs locally from Derbyshire to Northumberland, and the *artaxerxes* form is widely distributed in the Scottish Highlands.

Habitat. Flies in company with several species of blue butterflies on chalk downs, rough hillsides and grassy slopes, and on uncultivated meadows and waste-land.

Habits. Rapid fluttering flight over short distances only; feeds with wings spread open.

Life history. *Eggs*: white, laid singly on the underside of rock rose leaves. *Caterpillar*: just under ½ in. Pale green and curiously humped, with a dull purplish-brown stripe down the back, sides marked with oblique, wavy dark green streaks. Below the spiracles runs a white line edged on either side by a pink streak. The skin is thickly covered with short whitish hairs. Hibernates on the underside of a leaf low down on the plant. Pupates on the ground beneath the food-plant, attached to the stem by a few silk threads. *Chrysalis*: pale creamy-yellow with a brownish-pink line along the back, and pinkish markings on its rough spiny surface. *Butterfly*: double brooded in England, single brooded in Scotland. First brood on the wing in May and June, second in late July, August and into September. In June and July in Scotland.

82

COMMON BLUE *Polyommatus icarus* Pl. 9

Description. Wing-span: $1\frac{1}{8}$ in. Sexes quite distinct. Male clear violet-blue with white fringes, and wings thinly outlined at the margins in black. Female dull brown usually relieved by a suffusion of violet-blue scaling over the basal half of both fore- and hind-wings. A chain of orange crescents runs round the margins of all four wings being especially prominent on the hind-wings; fringes brown. The underside colouring of the male is pale bluish-grey, and in the female pale coffee. The markings are similar in both sexes, a sprinkling of black dots, surrounded by white rings. Along the outer margins of the wings runs a chain of black spots followed by lines of white, orange and black crescents, far brighter in the female than in the male. Plate 9: fig. 4c, ab. *supracaerulea*, an 'all blue' female form found not uncommonly in Ireland. Specimens vary considerably in size.

Length of life. 10–14 days.

Distribution. Our commonest blue butterfly. Well distributed and common in most of Britain and Ireland.

Habitat. Fields and meadows, any rough pasture or waste-ground, hillsides and downland.

Habits. Quick fluttering flight low over the ground often alighting on grass stems to sun themselves with wings half open. Congregate in the evening and rest high up on grasses, with their heads towards the ground.

Life history. *Eggs*: greenish, laid singly on the upper surface of bird's-foot trefoil leaves, sometimes on restharrow or black medick. *Caterpillar*: $\frac{1}{2}$ in. Bright green with a darker line down the arched back and greenish-white stripes along the sides of the body. Skin rough and covered with white hairs, forming a fringe round the body. A honey gland on the tenth segment. Larvae of the second brood hibernate after the second moult on the food-plant, beginning to feed again in March or April. Pupates at base of plant in a rough silken cocoon. *Chrysalis*: greenish, with creamy-buff wing-cases; whole surface covered with tiny bristles. *Butterfly*: usually double brooded, first on the wing in late May and throughout June, second during August and September.

Description.   Wing-span: 1¼ in. Sexes quite distinct. Male light silvery-blue, fore-wing margins outlined in black, hind-wings carry a series of six black spots ringed with white and outlined in black. Long white fringes broken by black veins. Female dull brown, often dusted with blue scaling near the body, especially on the hind-wings which have a row of black marginal spots, edged with cream and orange crescents. Fringes cream, and brown veined. Male underside is pale greyish-blue on the fore-wing, with nine white-ringed black spots and edged with a chain of dark lunules, while the hind-wing carries about a dozen similar white-ringed black spots on a brownish-buff ground colour; the lunules round the outer margins are black, edged with orange crescents, outlined in white. Female underside similar, but dark coffee-coloured; the spots and lunules are usually larger and brighter than in the male. Plate 9: fig. 5c, a female with excess of blue scaling, not uncommon in some localities; fig. 5d, a colour form of a male with extra deep black marginal band on the fore-wings, rare; fig. 5e, a male with a chain of white spots in place of the black marginal band. Plate 8: fig. 7, underside, male, with two black spots at the base of the fore-wing extended into short streaks, not uncommon; fig. 7a, male underside, with the spotting on the hind-wing reduced to the single orbicular spot, and fore-wing spots reduced in number to three instead of the normal nine.
Length of life.   12–15 days.
Distribution.   Although less common than formerly, still to be found in large numbers in the chalk areas of south and south-west England. The most northern colony is in Lincolnshire.
Habitat.   Chalk and limestone hills and downs, where its food-plant grows and scrub has not encroached.
Habits.   Rather fast fluttery flight up and down the steep slopes of the downs, often settling with wings half open to feed from wild flowers.
Life history.   *Eggs*: white and flattened, laid singly on the stems of horse-shoe vetch. Overwinters in this stage, hatching seven months later. *Caterpillar*: ½ in. Fresh green, resembling a woodlouse in shape, marked with clear yellow stripes on each side of the back, and with stripes of the same colour running the entire length of the body on each side, just below the spiracles. A honey gland on the tenth segment. The skin is rough, sprinkled with tiny white hairs and spines. Pupates amongst rubbish on the ground. *Chrysalis*: dull brownish-yellow, speckled and marked with brown warts and short hairs; rounded at both ends. *Butterfly*: single brooded, emerging in late July and on the wing throughout August and well into September.

ADONIS BLUE *Lysandra bellargus*

Description. Wing-span: $1\frac{1}{8}$ in. Sexes differ. Male azure-blue
with the margins of all four wings edged with black; fringes white.
Female grey-brown, occasionally dusted with blue scaling near the
body. Small white spot on each fore-wing and a chain of faint orange
spots along the margin. The hind-wings are edged with a row of black
spots ringed with blue, followed by a row of orange crescents edged
with black. Underside ground colour is grey in the male and buff-
brown in the female with all wings liberally sprinkled with small
round black spots, ringed with white. In the male the wings are edged
with a chain of black spots outlined in white merging into grey
crescents on the fore-wing and orange crescents on the hind-wing;
in the female all these marginal crescents are coloured. Plate 8: fig. 6a,
a rare gynandrous female with streaks of male coloration on left fore-
and hind-wings; fig. 6b, an extreme example of a form with the spots
elongated into long black streaks. Plate 9: fig. 6c, an extremely rare
halved gynandromorph, left side male, right side female.

Length of life. Spring brood 2 weeks, autumn brood 15–20 days.

Distribution. In chalk areas in southern England, but far less
common than formerly. It has been found locally as far north as
Hertfordshire.

Habitat. Chalk and limestone hills and downs from Kent to
Cornwall.

Habits. Fast fluttering flight close to the ground, often pausing to
feed, with wings half open, from wild flowers.

Life history. *Eggs*: pale greenish-white, laid singly on the leaves
of horse-shoe vetch. *Caterpillar*: $\frac{2}{3}$ in. Woodlouse-shaped with a
humped back; clear green with two bright yellow stripes along the
back and one low down on each side, just above the legs. Second
brood larvae hibernate through winter beneath the leaves. Pupates on
the ground in a flimsy silken cocoon. *Chrysalis*: varies from ochreous-
buff to dull buff tinted with green. *Butterfly*: first brood emerge at
the end of May, second brood in late August.

Description. Wing-span: 1 in. Sexes quite distinct. Male deep purplish-blue with the fringes white; the female dark brown with often a small amount of dark blue scaling near the body. Underside markings similar: fore-wings decorated with an irregular line of six white-ringed black spots, and a similar series of eight on the hind-wings. Ground colour of the male pale greyish-white, of the female pale ochreous-brown.

Length of life. 10–14 days.

Distribution. Apparently always a rarity in Britain, and probably extinct here for at least a century. Found originally as far north as north Lincolnshire.

Habitat. Uncultivated fields and meadows where its food-plant grows; any specimens seen nowadays would almost certainly be rare vagrants from Europe.

Habits. Flight and behaviour similar to the Common Blue, which the male closely resembles in size and upperside colour, though the two can be distinguished fairly easily by the differing underside patterns.

Life history. *Eggs*: greenish-white, laid on the leaves of clover or kidney vetch. *Caterpillar*: pale green mottled with pale brown and with a darker green line down the back and along the sides. Hibernates over winter in a dried flower head of the food-plant. Pupates beneath a leaf, attached by the hind claspers to a pad of silk, and supported by a silk girdle round the middle. *Chrysalis*: brownish-green, speckled with brown dots. *Butterfly*: in Europe the first brood appears on the wing in late April or May, the second in July and August, and a third is still flying right into mid-October.

LARGE BLUE   *Maculinea arion*   Pl. 10

Description.   Wing-span: $1\frac{1}{4}$ in. Sexes differ slightly. Male light greyish-blue with a narrow border of black round the margins and five or six elongated black spots on the fore-wings; hind-wings carry four faint dark spots ringed with white. Female slightly larger and a deeper violet-blue, the marginal bands broader, the spots on the fore-wings more numerous and elongated into short streaks. Undersides similar in both sexes: ground colour grey-buff diffused with bluish-green at the base of the wings, which are peppered with round black dots ringed with white. Plate 10: fig. 3c, rare variety ab. *insubrica*; fig. 3d, ab. *subtus-impunctata*; fig. 3e, male ab. *alconides*, a form with spotless forewings.

Length of life.   16–20 days.

Distribution.   Now one of our rarest indigenous butterflies, and apparently almost confined to north Devon, though it might survive in small numbers in Cornwall and the Cotswolds.

Habitat.   Rare and very local, rough grass pastures near coastal headlands, hillsides and valleys where gorse and heather grow, and where there are ants' nests covered with wild thyme.

Habits.   Flutters from flower to flower when feeding, but has quite rapid flight when disturbed. The males can be seen quartering hill-sides and valleys, flying fast over quite long distances.

Life history.   *Eggs*: greenish-blue, laid on the flowers of wild thyme. *Caterpillar*: pink while young and feeding on thyme blossom; after the third moult it wanders away from the food-plant and is picked up by an ant and carried down into the nests. These insects find the larvae attractive because of the sweet liquid which exudes from their honey glands. From then on the caterpillars remain in the ants' nests, feeding carnivorously on ant grubs in the underground galleries and becoming white and grub-like. Pupates in June, suspending itself from the roof of a chamber by its hind-claspers, attached to a silken pad. *Chrysalis*: pale yellow, gradually darkening to dark brown. *Butterfly*: emerges in total darkness and crawls through the galleries up to the light before commencing to dry its wings; usually clings to a sprig of gorse for this process. Emerges late in June or early in July, and on the wing into early August.

Description. Wing-span: $1\frac{1}{8}$ in. Sexes differ. Male soft lavender-blue with all four wings narrowly edged with black. Fringes white, spotted with black on the fore-wings. Female similar ground colour but the fore-wings have a wide black margin: the hind-wings have a row of black spots ringed with white and a wide black streak which runs the length of the front edge out to the margin. The second, or autumn brood, females are more heavily banded and marked with black than the spring brood. Underside similar in both sexes; pale greyish-blue speckled with black dots. Plate 10: fig. 4c, female, second brood form.

Length of life. 14–16 days.

Distribution. Well distributed and often common in England and Wales, but more subject to fluctuation in numbers than most butterflies. Also locally in Ireland, but not in Scotland.

Habitat. A garden and park butterfly where holly and ivy are grown, also in country lanes and open woodland and forest.

Habits. Likes to flutter around tall trees, frequently resting, with wings closed, on a leaf. The females can be seen hovering around holly bushes in spring and clumps of ivy in late summer.

Life history. *Eggs*: pale blue-green, laid in the spring on the flower-heads of holly or dogwood, in the summer on unopened buds of ivy blossom. *Caterpillar*: mainly green, but very variable, with purplish-pink and white lines, or pink and cream, or plain green with a yellow lateral line along the body. The back is arched, the head black and shining, and the body short and plump. The caterpillar attaches itself, limpet-like, to the flower bud and burrows its head right inside, eating all the substance until the bud is a hollow shell. Later eats the holly berries and dogwood fruits. It spins a pad of silk underneath a leaf before pupating, and attaches itself securely with a girdle of silk. *Chrysalis*: brownish-buff, smooth and rounded at both ends and speckled with brown marks. Overwinters in this stage. *Butterfly*: those in overwintering chrysalids emerge in mid-April. Second brood emerges in late July and during August.

SMALL COPPER   *Lycaena phlaeas*   Pl. 10

Description.   Wing-span: 1 in. Sexes similar. Fore-wings brilliant coppery-red marked with eight square black spots; a wide black band runs along the margin. Hind-wings grey-black, with scattered copper scales near the body, and a wide copper band round the margin spotted along the edges with black. Underside pale orange on the fore-wings with the pattern of black spots on the upperside repeated; hind-wing colouring light biscuit, faintly spotted with grey and the margins encircled with a chain of red crescent-shaped marks. This is a very variable butterfly. Plate 10: fig. 2c, ab. *caeruleopunctata*, a blue-spotted form, not uncommon; fig. 2d, ab. *fasciata*, spots on fore-wing elongated into streaks, rather rare; fig. 2e, ab. *fuscata*, dusky form; fig. 2f, ab. *bipunctata*, twin-spotted form, rare; fig. 2g, ab. *schmidtii*, colour form, ground colour pale straw, rare; fig. 2h, a form showing homoeosis, upperside markings transposed on to underside, very rare.

Length of life.   16–21 days.

Distribution.   Widely distributed and in some years very common in much of Britain and Ireland. Hot summers usually suit this species.

Habitat.   Waste-land, heaths, commons, meadows, fields, rough hillsides and downland.

Habits.   Quick fluttering flight. Has the habit of selecting a certain flower-head as a perch and making excursions from this to chase other butterflies or small insects from its chosen territory. Basks in the sun with wings half open.

Life history.   *Eggs*: pale greenish, laid singly on the leaves of dock or sorrel.   *Caterpillar*: ⅝ in. Either dark-green or yellowish-green, sometimes with a pink line along the back and a stripe of the same colour down the side of the body. Skin rough and covered with bristly brown hair. Spends the winter in partial hibernation lying in a groove which it eats out from the cuticle of a leaf. Feeds intermittently in mild weather. Pupates in late April.   *Chrysalis*: light brown, speckled with darker brown marks and spots, with a darker line down the back; plump in shape and attached to its food-plant by a silken girdle round the waist.   *Butterfly*: emerges in mid-May. Second brood on the wing during July, a third in September and into October.

Description.   Wing-span: male 1¼ in., female 1½ in. Sexes differ. Male rich iridescent coppery-red with black margins round all four wings. There are two black elongated spots near the centre of each fore-wing, and the inner margin of the hind-wing is suffused with black. The marginal black border is wider in the female and the two spots are enlarged into square blotches; a row of black spots runs transversely across the wing, inside the marginal band. Hind-wings are brownish black with veins etched in copper shade, and there is a copper band along the margin, which is edged with a scalloped black band. Undersides similar in both sexes: fore-wings coppery-red with a blue-grey band along the margin, edged on the inside with small black crescents, liberally speckled with black spots, outlined in white. Hind-wings pale ice-blue with a marginal band of coppery-red marked with black at the edges and similarly dotted with black spots, encircled with white.

Length of life.   14–18 days.

Distribution.   The butterflies are very similar to the extinct original British large coppers, and only survive here because of constant protection. They are confined to Wood Walton Fen, Huntingdonshire, where the species was introduced in 1927.

Habitat.   Over sedges and bogs in the Fens.

Habits.   Rapid flight over short distances, frequently settling on wild flowers with wings spread wide open.

Life history.   *Eggs*: white, laid singly on the leaves of water dock. *Caterpillar*: just over ¾ in. Soft green with a darker line along the back and sloping stripes along the sides. Woodlouse-shaped, with a humped back, the body covered with raised white dots. Becomes purplish-brown marked with green and hibernates in a furrow made by eating the cuticle from a leaf. Resumes green colouring in spring. Pupates beneath a leaf, attached by a silken girdle and a pad. *Chrysalis*: two shades of brown, speckled with dark raised spots and white warts.   *Butterfly*: single brooded; on the wing from late June until early August.

GREEN HAIRSTREAK *Callophrys rubi* Pl. 11

Description. Wing-span: 1 in. Sexes identical except for a small oval spot of black scent scales on the fore-wing of the male. Colouring of upperside rich bronze-brown, hind-wings scalloped and forming a short tail at the anal angle, flanges near body pale dingy-cream. Underside green with a grey area near the inner edge of the fore-wings and a white dotted line extending across the hind-wings. Plate 11: fig. 5b, a minor variety ab. *inferopunctata*, where the white dots are enlarged into white dashes.

Length of life. 14–18 days.

Distribution. Our commonest and most widely spread hairstreak. Found locally and often commonly in much of Britain and in some areas in Ireland.

Habitat. Hedgerows bordering woodland, country lanes, shrubby common heathland, hillsides and downs overgrown with scrub; on the moors in Scotland.

Habits. Performs extraordinary aerial acrobatics. Usually returns to the same perch, a hawthorn leaf, to rest in the sun after making a flight. Never strays more than a hundred yards or so from its home ground.

Life history. *Eggs*: greenish-white, laid singly on buds of dogwood, broom, gorse, bramble, etc.; on bilberry in Scotland. *Caterpillar*: $\frac{5}{8}$ in. Bright green with a row of oblique yellow streaks along each side and a stripe of the same colour running low down on the body. The back is arched, and the skin is covered with short brownish hair. Before pupating the fully-grown caterpillar wanders away from its food-plant and crawls down to the ground to pupate amongst litter at the foot of a bush. *Chrysalis*: plump and brown, finely covered with dark spines and streaked with black marks. Pupal stage lasts from July until early the following May. *Butterfly*: on the wing during May and the first half of June.

Description. Wing-span: 1¼ in. Sexes differ. Male brownish-black, with a short black streak next to a light creamy-yellow patch near the centre of the fore-wing. The margin of the hind-wing is slightly scalloped and has a short brownish tail and an orange-brown blotch at the angle of the wing. Female rich dark brown, with wide tawny-orange band across the fore-wings and a dark streak similar to the male; tail on hind-wings slightly longer and more curled and the orange blotch is larger. Underside similar in both sexes: light orange-brown ground colour with a small black streak and a wedge-shaped brown bar, edged with white, across the fore-wing. Hind-wing crossed by a broad irregular brown band, outlined in white, with a narrow band of orange along the margin. The body and legs are conspicuously white.

Length of life. 14–18 days.

Distribution. Formerly more widely distributed and common in suitable places as far north as Huntingdon. Now commonest in southern England, but found locally in a small area in western Ireland.

Habitat. A woodland species where blackthorn thickets exist; often seen feeding from bramble blossom.

Habits. Rather fast fluttering flight, settling frequently, with wings closed, on bramble blossom to feed on nectar. Keeps strictly to a small area in the home wood.

Life history. *Eggs*: white, streaked with grey; laid singly on black-thorn shoots, usually at the base of a bud. Overwinters in this stage from September to April, hatching early in the month when the trees come into leaf. *Caterpillar*: ¾ in. Clear green, with each segment sharply defined; back humped and sides and underneath rather flattened so larva appears triangular when seen from the front or rear. Body marked with two rows of yellow sloping stripes, a line of the same colour runs along the back, and another low down on each side, beneath the spiracles. Becomes purplish and then pupates, attached to its larval skin and fixed by a few silk threads to a leaf or stem of its food-plant. *Chrysalis*: ochreous brown, speckled with darker marks, compact in shape and rounded at both ends. *Butterfly*: single brooded; on the wing in August and September.

PURPLE HAIRSTREAK   *Quercusia quercus*   Pl. 11

Description. Wing-span: $1\frac{1}{4}$ in. Sexes distinct. Male greyish-black with a purplish sheen and black borders. Female velvety-black with a brilliant iridescent purple patch on the basal half of the fore-wings, hind-wings black, tinged with bronze. Both sexes carry a short tail on the hind-wing. Underside of both sexes similar: ground colour light-grey with a row of dark grey spots along the edge of the fore-wings, followed by a white line, bordered with brown. The hind-wings also have a white zig-zag line across them, and near the tail there is a dark brown line and spots of orange and black; above these is a larger black spot ringed with orange.

Length of life. 14–18 days.

Distribution. Widespread in wooded areas of southern England and extending into Wales and the Lake District. Found locally in parts of Scotland and Ireland.

Habitat. In woodland glades and on the outskirts of wooded country.

Habits. Dancing, fluttering flight, usually rather high up around a branch of a favourite oak tree. Basks with wings wide open on a leaf.

Life history. *Eggs*: white, laid singly on twigs of oak, usually close to the base of next year's bud. Overwinters in this stage and hatches when the oaks burst into leaf. *Caterpillar*: $\frac{5}{8}$ in. Yellowish-brown with a black stripe edged with white down the back, the sides of the body marked with bold, dark-brown streaks, bordered above with light cream. A narrow whitish-yellow line runs low down on each side, and the caterpillar is curiously flat in appearance. Bores into the bud, surrounding it with strands of silk. Pupates in June. *Chrysalis*: dark reddish-brown, speckled and marked with brown; thick and rounded at both ends. Hidden under moss or litter on the ground, and protected by a few strands of silk. *Butterfly*: on the wing during late July and August.

WHITE-LETTER HAIRSTREAK   *Strymonidia w-album*

Pl. 11

Description.   Wing-span: $1\frac{1}{8}$ in. Sexes differ slightly. Ground colour dark brownish-black. Male has a pale grey oval spot near the front edge of the fore-wings; hind-wings scalloped, with a short tail. Female has a rather longer tail and a distinct orange spot at the angle of the hind-wing. Underside pattern and markings similar in both sexes: ground colour light grey, with an irregular white line across the fore-wing; hind-wing marked with a similar line which is shaped to form the letter W. There is a large velvety black spot at the angle of the wing, followed by several smaller ones along the edge. A bright orange-red band, edged inside with a wavy black line, borders the margin.

Length of life.   14–18 days.

Distribution.   Common locally in southern England and extending northwards to south Yorkshire. Not in Scotland or Ireland.

Habitat.   In open woodland and country lanes; colonies sometimes found round isolated wych elm trees in the middle of a field.

Habits.   Rapid fluttering flight over short distances, often settling on the leaves of elm or to feed from bramble blossom. Never stray far from the breeding ground.

Life history.   *Eggs*: green at first, becoming dark brown. Laid singly on twigs of wych elm or common elm. Overwinters in this stage, hatching in March. *Caterpillar*: $\frac{7}{8}$ in. Light green, with a yellow stripe along the back and sloping yellow lines along the sides. Sometimes the ground colour is creamy-buff with pinkish stripes. The back is arched, with a groove down the middle. Feeds on elm flowers when young, and then the leaf buds, burrowing right inside. Becomes brownish and then pupates on a twig or underneath a leaf, held in position with a girdle of silk. *Chrysalis*: light brown marked with purplish-black spots and streaks. *Butterfly*: emerges in mid-July and on the wing for the first half of August.

Description. Wing-span: $1\frac{1}{8}$ in. Sexes differ slightly. Male dark brown with a series of three orange crescent-shaped marks on the hind-wings, and a short black tail with a white tip. Female: similar colouring but the orange spots on the hind-wings are larger and more numerous; fore-wings also carry a row of orange marks along the margin. Underside similar in both sexes: golden-brown with a curved line of white dots running across the fore-wings and continuing on the hind-wings to form an incomplete 'W'; a wide orange band of spots, bordered with black and silvery marks surrounds the margins of all four wings.

Length of life. 14–18 days.

Distribution. Another of our rarer indigenous butterflies. In a few woods where blackthorn grows freely in Huntingdonshire, Northamptonshire and Oxfordshire. Has been introduced into a few other areas, but not very successfully.

Habitat. Flies along the margins of woods and in clearings where blackthorn grows.

Habits. A very local butterfly, fluttering around blackthorn bushes and fond of visiting the flowers of wild privet to feed on the nectar. Always rests with wings closed.

Life history. *Eggs*: brown, laid singly on twigs of blackthorn. Overwinters in this stage, hatching into a caterpillar just as the buds are bursting into leaf in spring. *Caterpillar*: $\frac{5}{8}$ in. Pale green, with a humped back, grooved along the centre; marked with a double row of purplish-red marks along the back and low down on each side. Each segment is also marked with two yellow oblique stripes and the skin is lightly covered with short brown hairs. As well as eating young leaflets, they will eat each other. *Chrysalis*: ochreous brown with lighter patches on the sides and wing-cases; blotched and speckled with white. Closely resembles a bird dropping in shape and colouring. Pointed at head and tail and attached to a twig by a pad of silk and a girdle. *Butterfly*: single brooded, on the wing from the end of June into July.

Plate 13

1 **Black-veined White**, *Aporia crataegi* (p. 99) ♂ (sexes differ slightly) × $\frac{2}{3}$
1a underside ♂ × $\frac{2}{3}$
1b ♀ × $\frac{2}{3}$

2 **Bath White**, *Pontia daplidice* (p. 103) ♂ (sexes differ)
2a underside ♂
2b ♀

3 **Orange-tip**, *Anthocharis cardamines* (p. 104) ♂ (sexes differ)
3a underside ♂
3b ♀
3c ♂ ab. *aureoflavescens*
3d ♀ gynandrous form

4 **Wood White**, *Leptidea sinapis* (p. 105) ♂ (sexes differ slightly)
4a underside ♂
4b ♀

Scale: All butterflies on this plate are life size except the Black-veined White.

The Black-veined White is now almost certainly extinct in Britain, but fresh attempts to re-introduce it are constantly being made by amateur collectors and nature lovers. The Bath White is a rare and occasional migrant, usually only one or two making an appearance in any season, but in 1945 they invaded south and south-west England in very large numbers, and succeeded in establishing themselves for at least one generation. The Orange-tip is widely distributed throughout the British Isles and is subject to considerable variation; yellow instead of orange-tipped specimens sometimes occur (fig. 3c) especially in the Isle of Man. Albino forms and gynandrous specimens are also occasionally seen (fig. 3d). The Wood White is rather a local insect with a range restricted to some six or seven counties in the southern half of Britain; it also occurs in Ireland as subsp. *juvenica* Williams.

Plate 14

1 **Pale Clouded Yellow**, *Colias hyale* (p. 107) ♂ (sexes quite distinct)
1*a* underside ♂
1*b* ♀

2 **Berger's Clouded Yellow**, *Colias australis* (p. 108) ♂ (sexes differ)
2*a* underside ♂
2*b* ♀

3 **Clouded Yellow**, *Colias crocea* (p. 106) ♂ (sexes differ)
3*a* underside ♂
3*b* ♀

4 **Brimstone**, *Gonepteryx rhamni* (p. 109) ♂ × $\frac{2}{3}$ (sexes differ)
4*a* underside ♂ × $\frac{2}{3}$
4*b* ♀ × $\frac{2}{3}$

Scale: All butterflies on this plate are life size, except the Brimstone.

The Pale Clouded Yellow does not migrate to these shores with anything like the regularity of the Clouded Yellow, which appears in varying numbers during most seasons. When it does arrive here the females usually do not travel far and so local colonies may build up along the coastal districts from Thanet to Cornwall, wherever lucerne fields are in cultivation. The range of Berger's Clouded Yellow appears to be very limited and most of the authentic specimens have been captured on the hills behind Folkestone and in Thanet. Being a migrant, however, the species might appear anywhere in southern England. In some years Clouded Yellows cross the Channel in tens of thousands in June and July, and then by late August or early September the clover and lucerne fields are 'alive' with these butterflies and entomologists speak of a 'Clouded Yellow Year'. All three species usually perish in Britain when the cold of autumn begins, for they are continuously brooded in their native haunts, the Mediterranean regions. The Brimstone hibernates as a live butterfly and usually appears on the wing early in April. It is widely distributed; gynandrous varieties are very striking, e.g. when a pale greenish-white female is found to have streaks of the brilliant sulphur yellow of the male splashed across its wings.

Description. Wing-span: male $2\frac{3}{4}$ in., female 3 in. Sexes similar. Ground colour primrose-yellow marked with a bold black pattern. Fore-wings have wide black bands parallel to the margin, bordered with a row of yellow spots; basal area black, three black bars along the front edge, veins outlined in black. Hind-wings have the black band heavily dusted with blue scales; red eye-spot at the angle of the wing, margin bordered with yellow crescents and extending into a prominent black pointed tail. Underside similar in pattern and colouring but the dark bands are thickly dusted with yellow scales; wedge-shaped red marks edging the band on the hind-wing. Plate 12: fig. 1b, ab. *obscura*, a melanic specimen, very rare indeed.

Length of life. 18–21 days.

Distribution. Now confined to the Norfolk Broads area where it is given a measure of protection. Formerly at Wicken Fen in Cambridgeshire.

Habitat. Confined to the Norfolk marshes.

Habits. Vigorous flapping flight a few feet above the reed-beds; occasionally spirals into the sky on courtship flights. Feeds, with wings spread wide, on wild flowers.

Life history. *Eggs*: yellow, turning to rich mahogany after two days, laid singly on leaflets of hog's fennel. *Caterpillar*: $2\frac{1}{4}$–$2\frac{1}{2}$ in. When small, black with a white saddle mark on its back. Fully grown it assumes warning colours of vivid green, with a band of black dotted with orange spots on each segment. A forked orange tubercle in the shape of a Y is concealed in the first segment behind the head; it can be protruded at will when danger threatens and emits a pungent odour. Pupates over winter low down on a reed-stem in an upright position, held firmly by a girdle of silk round the waist and anal hooks secured to a silken pad. *Chrysalis*: two distinct colour forms, yellowish with green markings, or buff with dark brown streaks. *Butterfly*: emerges late May. In some years a small percentage emerge near the end of August, producing a second brood of caterpillars.

BLACK-VEINED WHITE *Aporia crataegi* Pl. 13

Description. Wing-span: $2\frac{1}{2}$ in. Sexes differ slightly. Male is white with the veining strongly marked with black scaling; along the outer edge of the fore-wings there is a row of dark triangles forming a band. Female has a semi-transparent appearance due to thin scaling, and the veining is brown. The underside markings are a repetition of the upperside, except that the wings are sparsely speckled with black scales.

Length of life. 10–14 days.

Distribution. Apparently extinct in Britain since the 1920s, but formerly found locally in several areas in southern England including the Isle of Thanet, Kent, its last stronghold here. Attempts to re-establish the species in this country seem to have failed.

Habitat. Wild countryside where blackthorn thickets abound.

Habits. Very local, straying only short distances from the home ground. Slow flapping flight, but will soar high into the air if disturbed. Basks with wings half open, rests with them closed.

Life history. *Eggs*: yellow, laid in small batches in leaves of blackthorn or whitethorn. *Caterpillar*: $1\frac{1}{2}$ in. Gregarious in the early stages, living in a thick web spun in the fork of a branch or twig and coming out to feed on a terminal shoot during the day. Furry and black, with a bright orange band speckled with black along the back. The under-surface of the body is a shining grey. Overwinters as a small hibernating caterpillar in colonies of a dozen to twenty-five. Pupates on the food-plant, supported by a girdle of silk. *Chrysalis*: easily mistaken for that of the Large White butterfly, having a cream or yellowish ground colour, mottled with black streaks and dashes. *Butterfly*: on the wing in early July.

Description. Wing-span: $2\frac{1}{4}$ in. Sexes differ. Male creamy-white ground colour with a deep black margin at the tip of the fore-wing, and a single black spot on the outer edge of the hind-wing. Female has two large black spots near the middle of the fore-wing and a black bar close by, and the spot on the hind-wing is in the same place as in the male but is more pronounced. On the underside both sexes are marked with two black spots near the middle of the fore-wing, and the hind-wings are pale yellowish-buff dusted with black scales.

Length of life. 12–16 days.

Distribution. Found in much of Britain, but numbers fluctuate from year to year. Also in Ireland. The native stock is frequently increased by the arrival of immigrants from Europe.

Habitat. Favours allotments and kitchen gardens, and fields where cabbages are grown commercially.

Habits. Restless nature, uneven flapping flight with frequent changes of direction, feeds from flowers with wings closed.

Life history. *Eggs*: yellow, laid in batches of anything from 20 to 50 on the under-surface of a cabbage leaf, horse-radish, turnip, various cresses and also nasturtium. *Caterpillar*: $1\frac{3}{4}$ in. Gregarious, feeding when young in a tight cluster on the underside of a leaf and eating only the green cuticle; later the colonies split up into small groups. Colour greenish-grey blotched with black, covered with small warts which are slightly hairy; three yellow longitudinal strips run the length of the body, one along the back and the other two along the sides. Pupates away from the food-plant, usually on a wall, fence, windowledge or tree-trunk. Many fail to pupate because they are attacked by a parasitic ichneumon fly which lays its eggs in the caterpillars, eventually killing them. *Chrysalis*: greenish-white, speckled with black markings and attached to its resting surface by a pad of silk and a girdle round the middle. Overwinters in this stage. *Butterfly*: first brood emerges in mid-April, the second brood in early August, and the species is on the wing late into September.

SMALL WHITE *Pieris rapae*

Pl. 12

Description. Wing-span: 1¾ in. Sexes distinct. Male is white with black tips and a black spot near the centre of each fore-wing; hind-wings carry another black spot on the front edge. Female pale yellowish-buff with dark tips, two black spots with a bar on the fore-wings and a single black dot on the hind-wings. At the base of the wings, connecting with the body, there is a powdering of black scales, more heavy in the female than the male. Underside similar in both sexes, fore-wings white with two black spots and a yellowish-buff tip, hind-wings rich creamy-yellow dusted with greyish scales. Summer brood more heavily marked and spotted and, in the female, richer buff ground colouring.

Length of life. 10–14 days.

Distribution. Usually common, and sometimes very abundant in most of Britain. Also in Ireland.

Habitat. Gardens and parks, market gardens where fields of cabbages are cultivated, the countryside generally.

Habits. Flapping erratic flight; several males will often give chase to a female and spiral upwards to a height of twenty or thirty feet. Males settle with wings half open, females with wings spread wide open and body half-raised in a 'display' attitude.

Life history. *Eggs*: pale yellow, laid singly on the under-surface of cabbage leaves. *Caterpillar*: 1 in. Pale green, with a yellow line along the centre of the back and broken lines of yellow dots and dashes along the sides; body coated with short greyish hairs. Generally leaves the cabbage plant to pupate, spinning a pad of silk on a wall or garden fence and secured in an upright position with a girdle of silk round the waist. *Chrysalis*: varies in colour from pale green through buff to dull grey, speckled with black dots and streaks. *Butterfly*: over-winters in the chrysalis stage, first brood emerging in early April, second brood in July.

Description.   Wing-span $1\frac{3}{4}$ in. Sexes differ. The male is white with black tips, has a single black spot near the centre of each fore-wing, and a smaller black spot on the edge of the hind-wing. The female is creamy-white, with twin spots and a black bar along the inner margin of the fore-wing; the black spot on the edge of the hind-wing is larger than in the male. Underside colouring in both sexes rather similar. The nervures or veins are well marked and dusted with black scales on a greenish-yellow ground, giving a 'green-veined' appearance. In the female the hind-wings are often a rich yellow and less heavily veined than in the male. Plate 12: fig. 4c, female variety ab. *confluens*, with the spots on the fore-wings united into a black band; fig. 4d, male ab. *sulphurea*, with ground colour citron-yellow, a form originally found wild in Ireland; fig. 4e, rare female ab. *aurea*, with pinkish-buff suffusion on fore-wings and buff-tinted hind-wings. Seasonal and local forms are most pronounced in this species.
Length of life.   12–16 days.
Distribution.   Another very common butterfly in most of Britain and Ireland. The yellow form is found in the latter country.
Habitat.   Water meadows, marshland, along the margins of woods and in woodland glades, country lanes and fields.
Habits.   Restless flight, dodging about low over the grass and herbage, settling occasionally with wings half open to feed from flowers; flies on dull sunless days if the weather is warm. Visits gardens and parks.
Life history.   *Eggs*: pale greenish-white, laid singly on the leaves of various cruciferous plants including jack-by-the-hedge, charlock, horse-radish, rape and various cresses. *Caterpillars*: 1 in. Soft green with black spiracles outlined in bright yellow; covered with short white silky hairs. *Chrysalis*: very variable, from bright green to buff, generally matching its surroundings to a remarkable degree; often heavily speckled with black dots and dashes. Attached to a leaf or the stem of a plant by a pad of silk at the tail end, and a silk girdle round the waist. Overwinters in this stage. *Butterfly*: first brood emerges in April, second brood on the wing from mid-August into September.

Description. Wing-span: 1¾ in. Sexes differ. Male white except for a chequered black patch at the tip of each fore-wing and a square black spot near the middle. Female has two black spots on the fore-wings and a chequered pattern forming a partial band around the outer edges of the hind-wings. Underside hind-wings and fore-wing tips mottled in green and white.

Length of life. Spring brood 3 weeks, summer brood 21–30 days.

Distribution. A rare immigrant in Britain, but it appeared in large numbers in south-west England in 1945. Has also bred here occasionally, but never became established.

Habitat. The countryside generally, particularly in flowering clover or lucerne fields.

Habits. Fast flight, never more than a few feet above the ground, quite unlike the British White butterflies to which it is in no way related. Feeds from flowers with wings closed.

Life history. *Eggs*: at first yellow, turning orange before hatching; laid on the underside of the leaves of its food-plant – common hedge mustard or wild mignonette. *Caterpillar*: 1 in. Thin and narrow, greenish-grey with yellow lines on either side of the body, speckled with black dots. *Chrysalis*: similar to that of the Small White, pale lilac-grey tinted with buff and dotted with black spots and streaks, attached to food-plant by a silken girdle round the middle. Over-winters in this stage. *Butterfly*: emerges in southern Europe in March or early April, second brood in mid-summer.

Description. Wing-span: $1\frac{3}{4}$ in. Sexes quite distinct. Male has white ground colour with nearly a third of the fore-wings deep orange outlined with black at the tips. There is a black discoidal spot near the centre and a powdering of black scales near the body. Female lacks the orange, and the black tip is slightly wider and has streaks of white running through it. The underside markings present a beautiful mottled effect in moss-green and white, the orange of the male appearing in the same position on the fore-wing, but the tip is ochreous-green, not black. Plate 13: fig. 3d, is a gynandrous specimen, a female with a streak of male coloration on the right fore-wing, a rare insect.

Length of life. 12–16 days.

Distribution. Common and well distributed in much of England and Wales; in Scotland mainly in the north-east; in many areas in Ireland.

Habitat. Country lanes, margins of fields surrounded by hedges, marshy meadows and sunny pathways bordering woodland.

Habits. Rather weak fluttering flight, often turning back on its own tracks; rests frequently on wild flowers to feed on nectar.

Life history. *Eggs*: creamy-white, changing to deep orange within two days of being laid singly on or among the flowers of various cruciferous plants, such as jack-by-the-hedge, cuckoo flower, charlock, etc. *Caterpillar*: $1\frac{1}{4}$ in. Blue-green on the back, shading to leaf-green on the sides, with a white stripe low down on the body. *Chrysalis*: colour varies from green to buff and the shape is curiously elongated and crescent-shaped, resembling a ripe seed-pod of jack-by-the-hedge, and attached by a girdle of silk round the waist. Overwinters in this stage, attached to the dead stem of the plant where, because of its shape and colouring, it is well camouflaged. *Butterfly*: begins to emerge in late April or early in May and on the wing for the rest of the month.

WOOD WHITE *Leptidea sinapis* Pl. 13

Description. Wing-span: 1½ in. Sexes differ slightly. Both milky-white on the upper surface, with greyish-black oblong blotches at the tips of the fore-wings; in the male these marks are bolder and darker. Beneath this blotch there are, in the male only, two short grey lines following the veins. The shape of the wings is slightly different in the female, being more rounded at the tip than in the male. Underside fore-wings white, hind-wings clouded with grey in the central area up to the body, outer marginal area white.

Length of life. 10–12 days.

Distribution. Fairly common in some wooded areas of south and south-west England, also in Northamptonshire. Not in Scotland, but widespread in Ireland.

Habitat. Woodland rides and glades, wooded lanes not surfaced with tarmacadam.

Habits. Weak feeble flight, settling frequently on wayside herbage to rest with wings closed.

Life history. *Eggs*: yellow, laid singly on the under-surface of tufted vetch or other leguminous plants. *Caterpillar*: almost 1 in. Bright green, with a darker green line down the back and bright yellow stripes along the sides of the body. A flap of flesh at the hind end of the body overlaps and hides the rear legs. Always pupates on the food-plant in an upright position, supported by a thin girdle of silk round the middle. *Chrysalis*: light green with a reddish tip, the wing-cases outlined in pink. Overwinters in this stage. *Butterfly*: the main hatch is in mid-May, but occasionally in a hot summer there is a partial second brood on the wing in late July and early August.

Description. Wing-span: 2 in. Sexes differ. Male has rich orange-yellow ground colour with dark bands round the outer margins of all four wings. Black spot near the centre of each fore-wing and a larger orange one on the hind-wing. Female differs from the male in that the black bands are wider and are broken up by a series of yellow spots and streaks. Underside markings are similar in both sexes, the prevailing colour being greenish-yellow with a chain of pink dots running round the inner margins; a large figure-of-eight mark in the centre of the hind-wing is silver, outlined in pink.

Length of life. 14–20 days.

Distribution. A regular immigrant, but scarcer in recent years. Usually commonest in southern England and southern Ireland. In 1947 it was found nearly all over Britain. Breeds here sometimes, but never established.

Habitat. Fields and meadows, especially where lucerne and clover are being grown, hillsides and downland.

Habits. A restless butterfly, never settling for more than a few moments to feed from flowers; fast purposeful flight, seldom turning back on its tracks. Breeding colonies will, however, stay in a lucerne field for some days before dispersing.

Life history. *Eggs*: at first yellowish-white, turning pinkish-orange after two days, laid singly by the migrant females on the upper surface of clover and lucerne leaves. *Caterpillar*: nearly $1\frac{1}{2}$ in. Bright dark green, velvety to the touch because of the very fine, short silky hairs covering the body. Along each side is a band of colour made up of yellow and reddish-orange streaks. The spiracles are edged with white rings. Hibernates over winter in southern Europe, feeding up rapidly in the spring. Pupates underneath a leaf or on the stem of the food-plant, attached by the tail and supported by a silk girdle. *Chrysalis*: dark green above, shading to yellowish-green beneath; dotted with black markings. *Butterfly*: emerges in March in southern Europe, and as population pressure builds up, migration north begins, the first butterflies arriving in Britain in late May or June. Emerge from August onwards here, and on the wing until mid-October.

PALE CLOUDED YELLOW *Colias hyale* Pl. 14

Description. Wing-span: $1\frac{7}{8}$ in. Sexes quite distinct. Male prim-rose-yellow with a black orbicular spot on each fore-wing, and a rather larger orange one on the hind-wings. A deep black border, widest at the tip, broken by a few yellow streaks, runs round the fore-wings. A similar, but narrower, black band, partially obscured by a band of yellow blotches, encircles the hind-wings. The female has the same pattern but the ground colour is greenish-white. Underside colouring of the fore-wings is pale yellow with darker greenish-yellow tips, and a chain of reddish spots near the edge; hind-wings golden-yellow with the line of reddish spots repeated in the same position. There is also a prominent silver spot, shaped like a figure-of-eight, outlined in pink almost in the centre.

Length of life. 14–21 days.

Distribution. An immigrant species, rarely in large numbers and has been scarcer in recent years. Mainly in south-east England.

Habitat. In lucerne and clover fields, usually near the coast where they stay to breed after making the Channel crossing; males are more often seen further inland, flying fast over fields and meadows and on hillsides.

Habits. Fast erratic flight, frequently settling on flower-heads with wings closed. Males tend to rove further afield than females.

Life history. *Eggs*: pale yellow, laid singly on the upper surface of lucerne or clover leaves. Turn orange and then black, before hatching. *Caterpillar*: $1\frac{1}{4}$ in. Light green, lightly speckled with black and having a white line, broken by orange and yellow dots, along the sides. Spends the winter as a small hibernating caterpillar settled down on the mid-rib of a leaf or on the stem, and in southern Europe starts to feed very early in spring. *Chrysalis*: resembles a withered lucerne leaf in shape and colour. Greenish-yellow, dotted with black, attached by a silk girdle to the stem of the food-plant. *Butterfly*: in southern Europe brood succeeds brood during the season, and in good years the first immigrants may be seen in Britain from late May onwards. If migration occurs early in summer, the larvae have time to feed up and produce a second brood in about October. The larvae and pupae of later arrivals rarely survive the winter, but there are isolated records of successful overwintering and emergence in spring.

Description. Wing-span: $1\frac{7}{8}$ in. Sexes differ. Male primrose-yellow, with a black spot near the centre of each fore-wing, and another rather larger orange one on the hind-wings. Similar markings appear on the wings of the female but the ground colour is greenish-white. In both sexes the deep black border on the fore-wings is broken up by yellow or greenish-white spots and streaks. The hind-wings are almost clear, which is the chief difference between this species and the Pale Clouded Yellow. Underside colouring: fore-wings pale yellow with darker tips and a black spot corresponding to the upperside mark, hind-wings rich golden-yellow dusted with black scales, and with a prominent silver spot, shaped like a figure-of-eight, outlined in pink, also a chain of pink spots near the edge of the wing.

Length of life. 14–20 days.

Distribution. A rare immigrant found occasionally in south-east England, where it has bred on a few occasions.

Habitat. Downland in the south of England.

Habits. Fast erratic flight low over the ground; visits lucerne and clover fields for nectar and feeds with closed wings.

Life history. *Eggs*: pale yellow; laid on the leaves of the horse-shoe vetch *Hippocrepis comosa*, the only food-plant. *Caterpillar*: $1\frac{1}{4}$ in. Bluish-green, with a yellow line along the spiracles and two more on either side of the back. Down the length of the back there is a chain of square black marks, one on each segment. Hibernates over winter, beginning to feed in mid-March. *Chrysalis*: green, with a wide yellow band on either side; attached to the stem of the food-plant by a girdle of silk. *Butterfly*: emerges in May. Second brood on the wing during August and the early part of September.

Description.   Wing-span: $2\frac{1}{4}$ in. Sexes distinct. Male is bright
lemon yellow with a deep orange spot in the centre of each wing. The
tip of each fore-wing is slightly hooked and there is a vestige of a
tail halfway along the bottom of the lower wings. The female has
similar marks but the ground colour is greenish-white. In both sexes
the antennae are pink and rather short. Underside colouring is duller
with prominent veins giving a leaf-like effect.

Length of life. $10-10\frac{1}{2}$ months.

Distribution.   Widespread in England, and commonest in the
south, but also found as far north as Westmorland. Not in Scotland,
but found in a number of places in Ireland.

Habitat.   Seen most frequently flying along hedgerows in country
lanes, or in fields bordering woods, in open woodland glades and
ridings, or on wooded downland slopes.

Habits.   Steady purposeful flight across country, following hedgerows and margins of woods where buckthorn may be growing. Feeds
with wings closed.

Life history.   *Eggs*: greenish-white at first, turning bright yellow
and then deep grey before hatching. Laid singly on the under-surface
of buckthorn leaves, usually on a terminal shoot.   *Caterpillar*: $1\frac{1}{4}$ in.
Deep glossy-green along the back, merging into a bluish-green on the
sides with a white line running the length of the body along the
spiracles. Underneath, including the legs and claspers, it is a yellowish-green so the total effect is rather that of a shadow than a caterpillar as it lies along the mid-rib of a leaf.   *Chrysalis*: resembles a
folded buckthorn leaf in colour and shape to a remarkable degree.
Attached to a pad of silk by its hind claspers with a girdle of silk
supporting its body, it hangs in a horizontal position, often beneath a
leaf.   *Butterfly*: hibernates, usually in an evergreen bush or a clump
of ivy, from late September to mid-March, but continues to fly well
into June. The summer brood emerge in late July and these are the
butterflies that live right through the winter.

Description.   Wing-span: 1 in. Sexes differ slightly. In both species the ground colour of the fore-wings is dull grey-brown marked with two transverse lines of black spots, these enclose a band of grey and a number of irregular blotches and short lines on the basal half of the wing. In the male the basal half of the costal margin is folded back, and this distinguishes it from the female. The margins are outlined with dark streaks and edged with white spots. Hind-wings very dark; grey-black, faintly sprinkled with white dots and with a pronounced margin of dark spots ringed with white. Underside light golden-brown, with cream-coloured spots along the margins and sprinkled all over the wings.

Length of life.   10–12 days.

Distribution.   Commonest in southern England, but its range extends northwards to Yorkshire and Westmorland. Sparingly in north-east Scotland, and locally in Ireland.

Habitat.   Uncultivated pastures and meadows, commons and heaths, banks and hillsides, also on chalk and limestone downland.

Habits.   Swift zig-zag flight, backwards and forwards low over the ground; most difficult to follow. Basks on the bare ground, with wings spread wide. Rests at night or on dull days with wings folded like a moth, laid along the body, fore-wings completely covering the hind-wings.

Life history.   *Eggs*: yellow, laid singly on the leaves of bird's-foot trefoil. *Caterpillar*: $\frac{2}{3}$ in. Greenish-yellow, tapering at each end, densely covered with short pointed white hairs and spines. Over-winters as a fully fed caterpillar in a hibernaculum of leaves. This species, like other members of the family, has a curious comblike appliance on its last segment, just above the anal opening, by which the pellets of excrement are thrown outwards so that its resting-place does not become fouled. It spends more than ten months in the caterpillar stage, pupating in April in the same hibernaculum, without having eaten. *Chrysalis*: slim and pointed at the tail end, colour variegated in shades of brown, dull green and yellowish specks, always hidden from view inside a rough silken cocoon constructed from leaves of its food-plant and strands of silk. *Butterfly*: emerges in late April, and on the wing into mid-June.

Description. Wing-span: $\frac{7}{8}$ in. Sexes very similar. Ground colour black, suffused with grey at the base of the wings; in the male the basal half of the edge of the fore-wing is folded back. All four wings patterned with irregular white spots of varying size and shape, but less heavily marked on the hind-wings. Underside: fore-wings marbled in grey and black, dotted and streaked with white, hind-wings brownish-grey, similarly marked with white. Plate 15: fig. 2b, ab. *taras*, white spots on fore-wings elongated into thick streaks.

Length of life. 10–12 days.

Distribution. Common in southern England and about as far north as the Wash, sparingly in Lincolnshire and Yorkshire. Local though widespread in Wales.

Habitat. Any uncultivated pastures, the outskirts of woods, along woodland pathways and open glades, downland slopes and hillsides.

Habits. Rapid darting flight close to the ground, in a zig-zag pattern that is hard to follow. Settles frequently on the bare soil or on a flower, with wings spread wide.

Life history. *Eggs*: light green, laid singly on wild strawberry leaves. *Caterpillar*: $\frac{3}{4}$ in. Pale green with an olive-brown stripe down the back and alternate stripes of brown and pink along the sides. Skin covered with white hairs. Spins a shelter of silk on the surface of a leaf, coming out to feed on the cuticle. Later draws the edges of a leaf together to form a tube, in which it lives. Pupates in a rough silk cocoon between the stems of the food-plant. *Chrysalis*: very variable, mottled in brown and speckled with black, the whole being covered with a white powdery substance and short bristles. Remains in the pupal stage for nearly nine months. *Butterfly*: emerges in mid-May of the following summer, and on the wing during the early part of June.

Plate 15

1 **Dingy Skipper**, *Erynnis tages* (p. 110) ♂ (sexes differ slightly)
1a underside ♂

2 **Grizzled Skipper**, *Pyrgus malvae* (p. 111) ♂ (sexes very similar)
2a underside ♂
2b ♂ ab. *taras* Bergstr.

3 **Essex Skipper**, *Thymelicus lineola* (p. 115) ♂ (sexes very similar)
3a underside ♂
3b ♀

4 **Mazarine Blue**, *Cyaniris semiargus* (p. 86) ♂ (sexes differ)
4a underside ♂
4b ♀

5 **Small Skipper**, *Thymelicus sylvestris* (p. 116) ♂ (sexes differ slightly)
5a underside ♂
5b ♀
5c ♀ ab. *larenigra* Verity
5d ♀ ab. *pallida* Mosley

Scale: All the butterflies on this plate are life size.

The Dingy and the Grizzled Skippers are two of the earliest butterflies to appear on the wing in spring; the former spends the winter as a nearly fully fed caterpillar in hibernation, the latter as a chrysalis, sheltering in a folded leaf. There is a well-known form, ab. *taras* of the Grizzled Skipper, in which the white spots are run together to form short thick bars (fig. 2b). The Mazarine Blue has been presumed extinct for well over a century, but there is reason for thinking that it once bred in Dorset, near Cardiff in Wales and in a few other areas. It is illustrated here because it might appear again any time, as the result of an immigrant female laying eggs on the kidney vetch, its food-plant. The Essex and Small Skipper are very similar in appearance, but they differ in that the former passes the winter in the egg stage, while the latter hibernates as a caterpillar. The Essex Skipper is not confined to Essex, and has been found in several more eastern counties.

Plate 16

1 **Large Skipper**, *Ochlodes venatus* (p. 119) ♂ (sexes differ)
1a underside ♂
1b ♀

2 **Silver-spotted Skipper**, *Hesperas comma* (p. 118) ♂ (sexes differ)
2a underside ♂
2b ♀

3 **Chequered Skipper**, *Carterocephalus palaemon* (p. 114) ♂ (sexes differ slightly)
3a underside ♂
3b ♀

4 **Lulworth Skipper**, *Thymelicus acteon* (p. 117) ♂ (sexes differ slightly)
4a underside ♂
4b ♂, unnamed aberration resembling a ♀
4c underside ♀
4d ♀

Scale: All the butterflies on this plate are life size.

The Large Skipper is the commonest and best known of this family and can be found in open glades in woods, in meadows, on hillsides and along the grass verges of roads and lanes. The Silver-spotted Skipper is more local and more or less confined to the chalk hills and downs of southern England. It is often found in company with the Chalk-hill Blue butterfly. The Chequered Skipper has long been a very local species in England, and confined to a few woods in the vicinity of Peterborough. Unfortunately its numbers have dwindled very seriously in the last few years, and it may even now be extinct there. It is also found sparingly in a limited area in Inverness-shire. The Lulworth Skipper is, of course, named after the popular beauty spot in Dorset, and its limited range extends a short distance westwards from there. Skipper butterflies are not normally subject to much variation, though there are occasional exceptions.

CHEQUERED SKIPPER *Carterocephalus palaemon* **Pl. 16**

Description. Wing-span: 1 in. Sexes differ slightly. Male ground colour brownish-black, dusted with yellow scales; fore-wings chequered with square spots of deep yellow and suffused with yellow along the front edge and the base of the wing; hind-wings carry large round yellow spots and are edged with a row of streaks of the same colour. Female slightly larger, with lighter ground colour and paler spots and streaks, especially on the hind-wings. Underside markings similar to upper side, but paler on the fore-wings and the hind-wings are greyish-green heavily dusted with yellow scales.

Length of life. 10–14 days.

Distribution. Originally common in its few local haunts in Northamptonshire, Lincolnshire and Rutland, but has declined drastically in numbers in recent years and possibly now extinct. Also in a limited area in Inverness-shire.

Habitat. Woodland rides and glades.

Habits. Fast darting flight, fond of settling on wild flowers, particularly purple bugle, to feed on nectar. Basks in the sun with wings spread in the way characteristic of the Skipper family, fore-wings raised, hind-wings spread open.

Life history. *Eggs*: pearly white, laid singly on blades of false brome-grass. *Caterpillar*: green when young, striped lengthwise with light and dark lines. When fully grown it turns pale yellow, with a dull pink stripe down the back and a white line along the side. Spends the winter in a hibernaculum constructed of two blades of grass spun together to form a tube. Remains in this position from October to April, and then pupates. *Chrysalis*: pale yellow, flushed with grey and marked with reddish-brown lines. Slim, with pointed head and tapering tail. *Butterfly*: emerges in mid- to late May and on the wing the first half of June.

Description. Wing-span: 1 in. Sexes almost identical. Upperside colouring golden-brown with front edge of fore-wing and outer margins of both wings edged with narrow bands of black. Base of wings dull olive-brown. Male has a sloping line of black androconial scales on the fore-wing, which is absent in the female. Fringes black along the edge of wings and creamy-yellow at tips. Antennae brown on upper-surface and cream underneath, with black marks on the extreme tip of the under-surface, which is the distinguishing feature between this butterfly and the Small Skipper. Underside: fore-wings dark creamy-yellow suffused with dark grey from the base along the inner margin, hind-wings greyish, with a creamy patch at the angle and a band of the same colour along the front edge.

Length of life. 10–14 days.

Distribution. Especially in south-east England, and in smaller numbers as far north as Newark. Not in Wales, Scotland or Ireland.

Habitat. Rough pastures, canal banks and railway cuttings, hillsides, and downs.

Habits. Fast buzzing flight, but only over short distances. May be seen feeding from thistle flowers, resting with hind-wings spread and fore-wings slightly raised in the position characteristic of this family of small butterflies.

Life history. *Eggs*: at first pale yellow, later turning white; carefully inserted by the female on to the inner surface of the sheath of a blade of grass. Often laid in a row of five to six at a time. Laid in August but do not hatch until the following April, when the grass begins to sprout. *Caterpillar*: ⅞ in. Green, matching the grass on which it feeds, with a darker green line along the centre of the back. On each side of the slim tapering body there is a band of light yellow, spotted with green, and a distinct white line above the legs. Lives in a tubular shelter constructed by sewing together the edges of a blade of grass with silk threads. *Chrysalis*: pale green streaked with darker green and white; slender, with a pointed tail and rather thick rounded head bearing a beak-like horn. Hidden from view in a cocoon of silk spun among several blades of grass. *Butterfly*: emerges in late July and flies throughout August.

Description. Wing-span: male $\frac{7}{8}$ in., female 1 in. Sexes differ slightly. Ground colour light golden-brown shaded with olive-brown at the base of the wings. Fore-wings of the male carry an oblique line of scent scales from the centre to the hind margin; this is lacking in the female. Outer margins of all four wings outlined in black. Under-side ground colour pale creamy-yellow with a large wedge of olive-yellow covering half of the hind-wings. Antennae black on the upper-surface and cream-coloured underneath, with orange tips.

Length of life. 10–14 days.

Distribution. Common in much of England as far north as York-shire, also in south Wales and some other parts of that country, but not in Scotland or Ireland.

Habitat. Fairly widespread in woodland clearings, waste-ground, meadows and fields, or on hillsides and downland.

Habits. Rapid buzzing flight over short distances, settling on flower heads to feed with fore-wings raised and hind-wings spread out flat.

Life history. *Eggs*: pale yellow, laid several at a time in a small row, hidden from view in a sheath of grass. *Caterpillar*: $\frac{7}{8}$ in. Grass green, with a darker green line edged with pale yellow along the back, and a cream band marked with green dots along each side of the body. Lives in a tubular shelter constructed by drawing together the edges of a blade of grass with silk. Overwinters enclosed in a small cocoon of silk attached to a grass blade, beginning to feed again in April. Pupates early in July, attached to a grass stem by a girdle, hidden from view among a tangle of blades sewn together with silk. *Chrysalis*: green, flushed with pink, with a darker green stripe down the back; the surface covered with a waxy white bloom. *Butterfly*: emerges in July and on the wing during the early part of August.

LULWORTH SKIPPER *Thymelicus acteon* Pl. 16

Description. Wing-span: 1 in. Sexes differ only slightly. Ground colour of both sexes golden-olive, the male marked with a curved sloping narrow streak of black scent scales on the fore-wing and the female with a series of light-coloured marks which form a long narrow cell with a dark centre. Male underside a light sandy colour, heavily powdered with grey-green scales, female similar but more greyish-yellow. Plate 16: fig. 4b, a colour variety of a male heavily marked like a female; many males have faint markings on the fore-wings resembling the pattern of the female.

Length of life. 12–16 days.

Distribution. Very local, and more so than formerly, in the vicinity of Lulworth Cove and westward into south Devon.

Habitat. Flies on the downs near the coast, and on cliff-tops and in valleys between the downs.

Habits. Rapid flight, darting low over the turf and settling with fore-wings raised, hind-wings spread.

Life history. *Eggs*: yellow, laid in rows of five to fifteen inside the sheaths of grass, usually false brome-grass. *Caterpillar*: 1 in. Greenish-yellow, with a thin yellow stripe along the back, bordered on each side by a white band. Another broad white band edged with dark green is situated just above the legs. On hatching, spins a dense white cocoon and hibernates in this until late March or early April, when it starts to feed. Pupates in June. *Chrysalis*: grass green, with a dark green stripe running lengthwise, so that it resembles the grass blade on which it rests. Lies more or less hidden in a small tussock of grass spun together with silk. Has a long horn on the head. *Butterfly*: emerges in mid-July and on the wing during the first half of August.

SILVER-SPOTTED SKIPPER *Hesperia comma* Pl. 16

Description. Wing-span: 1⅜ in. Sexes differ. Male: golden-brown fore-wings with a darker broad band along the margins, marked with dull yellow spots near the tip. A wide patch of black scent scales is situated in the centre of the wing. Hind-wings brownish-grey, spotted with golden-brown. Female slightly darker with the base of the fore-wings flushed with golden-brown and an irregular row of square yellow spots across the wings; hind-wings carry five rather indistinct golden-brown spots. Underside of fore-wing green at the tip, spotted with cream, buff in the middle and black at the base. Hind-wings mustard-green spotted with white.

Distribution. Formerly well distributed on chalk downs of southern England and as far north as Hertfordshire, but more local and in reduced numbers today.

Habitat. Chalk and limestone hills and downs, and occasionally on waste-land in chalk country.

Habits. Fast flight, darting about from flower to flower. Basks in the sun with wings spread; rests at night with wings closed.

Life history. *Eggs*: white, later turning dark yellow, laid singly on blades of sheep's fescue grass. Overwinters in this stage, hatching in early April. *Caterpillar*: just over 1 in. Dull green with a black head. Covered with minute black warts from which grow short yellowish spines. Hides away in a shelter, close to ground level, made by spinning blades of grass together with silk. Pupates in July at ground level in a cocoon made by weaving together growing and bitten-off pieces of grass. *Chrysalis*: grey-green, slightly spotted with yellow at the tail end. Wing-cases covered with a thick waxy bloom. Numerous small hooks at both ends secure the pupa to the inside of the cocoon. *Butterfly*: emerges early in August.

LARGE SKIPPER *Ochlodes venatus* Pl. 16

Description. Wing-span: 1⅜ in. Sexes differ. Male fulvous-brown, with a sloping band of scent scales on the fore-wing and a series of orange-brown spots near the middle; hind-wings marked with some golden-brown spotting. Margins of all four wings edged with black, fringes yellow. Female slightly larger with more well-defined spotting and darker ground colour, inclining to olive-brown. Underside of both sexes similar: fore-wings creamy-yellow, shading to dull green at the tips and almost black at the base; hind-wings greenish-yellow, with a row of pale yellow spots parallel to outer margin and a wedge-shaped area tinted with orange along the hind margin.

Length of life. 12–16 days.

Distribution. The most widely spread of our Skipper butterflies. Common in much of England and Wales, but not in Scotland or Ireland.

Habitat. Woodland clearings and ridings, country lanes, uncultivated pasture, fields and meadows, and on hillsides and downs.

Habits. Very active, flitting about from flower to flower, frequently settling on grass stems or foliage to bask in the sun in the usual Skipper attitude, with fore-wings raised.

Life history. *Eggs*: pearly white, laid singly on grass blades. Later turn orange and then transparent white. *Caterpillar*: 1⅛ in. Green on the upper surface, greeny-blue beneath, with a darker green line along the back and yellowish line along the spiracles. After casting its fourth skin it goes into hibernation over winter, living in a tubular shelter constructed from a grass blade sewn together with silk. Begins to feed again in March. Pupates in May in a silken cocoon within a tent of grass blades previously spun together. *Chrysalis*: blackish-green, shading to grey-green; narrow and tapering towards the tail. Suspended by sharp spines and hooks on the head and tail. *Butterfly*: emerges in June and on the wing until mid-August.

MONTHLY LIFE HISTORY TABLES OF THE BRITISH BUTTERFLIES

Explanation of Symbols

E	= egg (ova)	B	=	butterfly (imago — perfect insect)
C	= caterpillar (larva)	HB	=	hibernating butterfly
Ch	= chrysalis (pupa)	Im	=	.immigrant (= migrant)

	Jan.	Feb.	Mar.	Apr.
Milkweed or Monarch				
Wall Brown	C	C	C	C
Speckled Wood	C or Ch	C or Ch	C or Ch	C,B,E
Mountain Ringlet	C	C	C	C
Scotch Argus	C	C	C	C
Marbled White	C	C	C	C
Grayling	C	C	C	C
Hedge Brown or Gatekeeper	C	C	C	C
Meadow Brown	C	C	C	C
Ringlet	C	C	C	C
Large Heath	C	C	C	C
Small Heath	C	C	C	C,Ch
Small Pearl-bordered Fritillary	C	C	C	C
Pearl-bordered Fritillary	C	C	C	C
Queen of Spain Fritillary				
Dark Green Fritillary	C	C	C	C
High Brown Fritillary	E	E	E,C	C
Silver-washed Fritillary	C	C	C	C
Heath Fritillary	C	C	C	C
Glanville Fritillary	C	C	C	C
Marsh Fritillary	C	C	C	C
Painted Lady				
Red Admiral				
Small Tortoiseshell	HB	HB	HB	HB,E
Large Tortoiseshell	HB	HB	HB	HB
Peacock	HB	HB	HB	HB
Camberwell Beauty				
Comma	HB	HB	HB	HB,E
Purple Emperor	C	C	C	C
White Admiral	C	C	C	C
Duke of Burgundy Fritillary	Ch	Ch	Ch	Ch
Long-tailed Blue				
Small Blue	C	C	C	C
Short-tailed Blue				
Silver-studded Blue	E	E	E	C
Brown Argus	C	C	C	C
Common Blue	C	C	C	C
Chalk-hill Blue	E	E	E	C
Adonis Blue	C	C	C	C
Mazarine Blue				
Large Blue	C	C	C	C
Holly Blue	Ch	Ch	Ch	Ch,B
Small Copper	C	C	C	C,Ch
Large Copper	C	C	C	C

Where more than one symbol is shown in any month, the stages overlap (i.e. the eggs are hatching into caterpillars, or the chrysalids are emerging as live butterflies.

May	Jun.	Jul.	Aug.	Sep.	Oct.	Nov.	Dec.
	Im	Im	Im	Im	Im		
Ch,B,E	B,E,C	C,Ch,B	B,E,C,Ch	B,C	B,C	C	C
B,E,C	Ch,B,E,	C,Ch	Ch,B,E	B,C	B,C or Ch	C or Ch	C, or Ch
C	Ch,B	B,E,C	C	C	C	C	C
C	C	C,Ch	B,E	C	C	C	C
C	C,Ch	Ch,B,E	B,E,C	C	C	C	C
C	C,Ch	Ch,B	B,E,	B,E,C	C	C	C
C	C	Ch,B	B,E,C	B,E,C	C	C	C
C,Ch	C,Ch,B	Ch,B,E	B,E,C	B,C	C	C	C
C	C,Ch	Ch,B,E,	B,E,C	C	C	C	C
C	Ch,B	B,E,C	C	C	C	C	C
B,E,C,Ch	B,E,C,Ch	B,E,C,Ch	B,E,C,Ch	B,E,C,Ch	B,C	C	C
C,Ch	B,E,	E,C,Ch	B,E,C	C	C	C	C
C,Ch,B	B,E,C,	C	C	C	C	C	C
Im	Im	Im	Im	Im	Im		
C	C,Ch	Ch,B	B,E	C	C	C	C
C	C	Ch,B,E	B,E	E	E	E	E
C	C,Ch	Ch,B,E	C	C	C	C	C
C	Ch,B	B,E	C	C	C	C	C
C,Ch,B	Ch,B,E	C	C	C	C	C	C
C,Ch,B	B,E	C	C	C	C	C	C
E, Im	E,C,Ch,Im	C,Ch,B,Im	E,C,Ch,B,Im	C,Ch,B,Im	C,Ch,B		
E, Im	E,C,Ch,Im	C,Ch,B,Im	E,C,Ch,B,Im	C,Ch,B,Im	C,Ch,B	B	
B,E,C	C,Ch,B	Ch,B,E	C,Ch,B	Ch,B	B	HB	HB
HB,E	C	C,Ch,B	B	HB	HB	HB	HB
HB,E	E,C	C,Ch,B	B	B	HB	HB	HB
Im	Im	Im	Im	Im	Im		
HB,E,C	C,Ch	Ch,B,E	C,Ch,B	B	B	HB	HB
C	C,Ch	Ch,B	B,E,C	C	C	C	C
C	C,Ch	B,E	B,E,C	C	C	C	C
Ch,B	B,E,C	C,Ch	Ch	Ch	Ch	Ch	Ch
		Im	Im	Im			
C,Ch,B	B,E	C	C	C	C	C	C
Im	Im	Im	Im	Im			
C	C,Ch	Ch,B,	B,E	E	E	E	E
Ch,B	B,E,C	C,Ch,B	Ch,B,E	B,E,C	C	C	C
Ch,B	B,E,	C	C,Ch,B	B,E,C	C	C	C
E	C	Ch,B	B,E	B,E	E	E	E
Ch,B	B,E,C	C	C,Ch,B	B,E,C	B,C .	C	C
Im	Im	Im	Im	Im			
E	C, Ch, B	B,E	B,E,C	C	C	C	C
Ch,B,E	B,E,C	C,Ch, B	B,E,Ch	C,Ch	Ch	Ch	Ch
Ch,B,E,C	B,E,C	Ch, B,E,C	Ch, B,E,C	Ch,B,E,C	B,E,C	C	C
C	C,Ch,B	B,E	B,E,C	C	C	C	C

MONTHLY LIFE HISTORY TABLES OF THE BRITISH BUTTERFLIES

	Jan.	Feb.	Mar.	Apr.
Green Hairstreak	Ch	Ch	Ch	Ch
Brown Hairstreak	E	E	E	E,C
Purple Hairstreak	E	E	E	E,C
White-letter Hairstreak	E	E	E,C	C
Black Hairstreak	E	E	E,C	C
Swallow-tail	Ch	Ch	Ch	Ch
Black veined White	C	C	C	C
Large White	Ch	Ch	Ch	Ch,B
Small White	Ch	Ch	Ch,B	B,E
Green-veined White	Ch	Ch	Ch	Ch,B
Bath White				
Orange-tip	Ch	Ch	Ch	Ch,B
Wood White	Ch	Ch	Ch	Ch
Clouded Yellow				
Pale Clouded Yellow				
Berger's Clouded Yellow	C	C	C	C,Ch
Brimstone	HB	HB	HB	HB
Dingy Skipper	C	C	C	C, Ch, B
Grizzled Skipper	Ch	Ch	Ch	Ch
Chequered Skipper	C	C	C	C,Ch
Essex Skipper	E	E	E	E,C
Small Skipper	C	C	C	C
Lulworth Skipper	C	C	C	C
Silver-spotted Skipper	E	E	E	C
Large Skipper.	C	C	C	C

May	Jun.	Jul.	Aug.	Sep.	Oct.	Nov.	Dec.
Ch,B	B,E	C	Ch	Ch	Ch	Ch	Ch
C	C	C,Ch	B	B,E	E	E	E
C	C,Ch	Ch, B,E	B.E.	E	E	E	E
C	C,Ch,	Ch, B	B,E	E	E	E	E
C	C,Ch,B	B,E	E	E	E	E	E
Ch,B	B,E,	C,	C,Ch,B,E.	C,Ch	Ch	Ch	Ch
C,	C,Ch	Ch, B,E,	E,C	C	C	C	C
Ch,B,E	C,Ch	C,Ch,B	B,E,C	E,C,Ch,B	B,C,Ch	Ch	Ch
B,E,C,	C,Ch,B	B,E,C	C,Ch,B	C,Ch,B	B,Ch	Ch	Ch
Ch,B,E	C	C,Ch	Ch,B,E	C,Ch	Ch	Ch	Ch
		Im	Im	Im			
Ch,B,E	B,E,C,	C	C,Ch	Ch	Ch	Ch	Ch
Ch,B,E	E,C	Ch,B,E	E,C	Ch	Ch	Ch	Ch
E,Im	E,C,Im	E,C,Ch,Im	B,E,C,Ch	B,C,Ch	B,C,Ch		
Im	E,C,Im	E,C,Ch,Im	E,C,Ch,Im	E,C,Ch,Im	C,Ch,B		
Ch, B,E	E,C	C,Ch	Ch,B,E	B,C	C	C	C
HB,E	HB,E,C	C,Ch,B	B	HB	HB	HB	HB
B,E	B,E,C	C	C	C	C	C	C
Ch,B	B,E,C,	C	C,Ch	Ch	Ch	Ch	Ch
Ch,B	B,E	C	C	C	C	C	C
C	C	Ch,B,E	B,E	E	E	E	E
C	C	Ch,B,E	B,E,C	C	C	C	C
C	C, Ch	Ch,B,E	B,E,C	C	C	C	C
C	C	C,Ch	B,E	E	E	E	E
C,Ch	B	B,E,C	B,E,C	C	C	C	C

INDEX

DISTRIBUTION MAPS

These very simplified maps are based on the provisional distribution maps issued by the Biological Records Centre, Monk's Wood, Huntingdon. They refer to the situation that existed about 1970, and should be used with caution. For example, the Small Tortoiseshell and its close relation the Large Tortoiseshell would seem from the maps to be equally well distributed throughout the British Isles. This is true up to a point, but whereas the Small Tortoiseshell is a common species, to be found almost wherever nettles (the food plant of its caterpillars) grow, the Large is decidedly local, rare and sporadic, although elms, its food plant, are (or were) among our commonest trees.

Hatched areas on the maps cover a variety of situations. In general they represent areas in which a species may be expected to occur, though probably rather rarely, in suitable habitats. They also indicate areas where a species used to occur but is unlikely to be found now, as in the case of the Purple Emperor, for example.

Scarce species with small localised populations should *on no account* be collected. Not all species are on the decline, however: the Comma, which seventy years ago was restricted to a very small area in the Wye Valley, has since spread throughout Wales and England up to the Scottish border. And the hot summers of 1975 and 1976 have shown how resilient some species can be, both in numbers and distribution, given favourable conditions.

Amongst the butterflies found in the British Isles are several that are not truly indigenous, their occurrence being due to a periodic influx of migrants and strays from the Continent. Some of these, for example the Red Admiral and Painted Lady, arrive annually with some regularity but in varying numbers. Others, like Clouded Yellows and the Camberwell Beauty (from Scandinavia) turn up in most years but usually in quite small numbers. The Queen of Spain Fritillary, the Long-tailed Blue and the Bath White are rarities of which there may be reports only at intervals of years. Most of these, if they arrive early enough, may produce broods that extend their range considerably. The Monarch (not mapped) is in a different category since there are no indigenous Milkweeds for its caterpillars to feed on. Distribution maps of these species only indicate in broad outline the areas in which, in the light of past experience, they are likely to turn up.

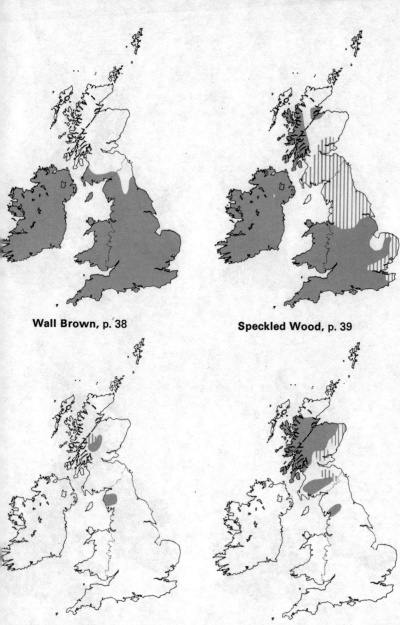

Wall Brown, p. 38

Speckled Wood, p. 39

Mountain Ringlet, p. 40

Scotch Argus, p. 41

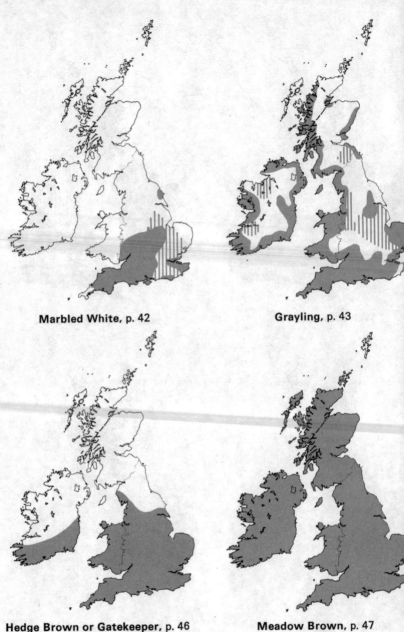

Marbled White, p. 42

Grayling, p. 43

Hedge Brown or Gatekeeper, p. 46

Meadow Brown, p. 47

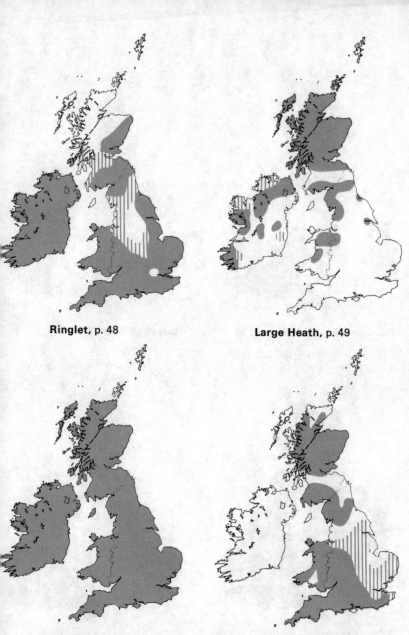

Ringlet, p. 48

Large Heath, p. 49

Small Heath, p. 50

Small Pearl-bordered Fritillary, p. 51

Pearl-bordered Fritillary, p. 54

Queen of Spain Fritillary, p. 55

Dark Green Fritillary, p. 56

High Brown Fritillary, p. 57

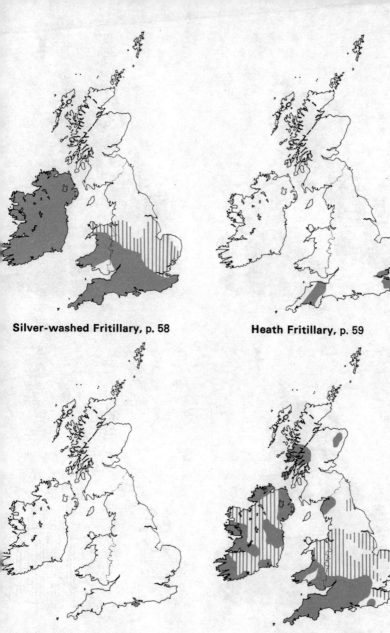

Silver-washed Fritillary, p. 58

Heath Fritillary, p. 59

Glanville Fritillary, p. 62

Marsh Fritillary, p. 63

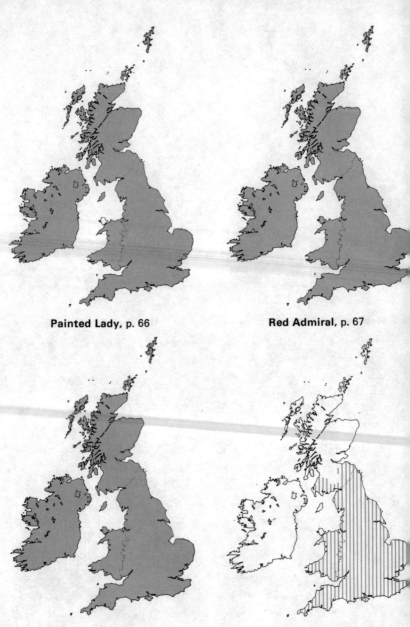

Painted Lady, p. 66

Red Admiral, p. 67

Small Tortoiseshell, p. 68

Large Tortoiseshell, p. 69

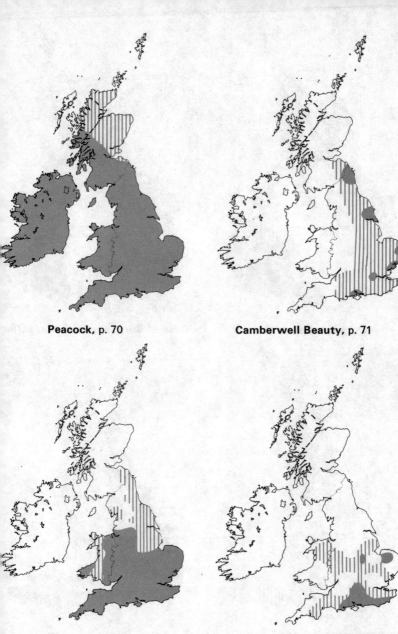

Peacock, p. 70

Camberwell Beauty, p. 71

Comma, p. 72

Purple Emperor, p. 73

White Admiral, p. 74

Duke of Burgundy Fritillary, p. 75

Long-tailed Blue, p. 76

Small Blue, p. 77

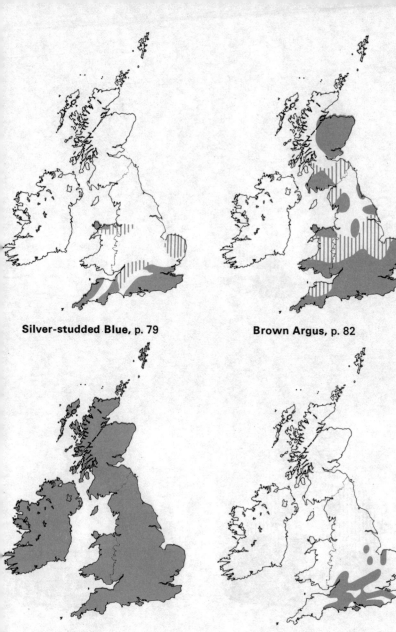

Silver-studded Blue, p. 79

Brown Argus, p. 82

Common Blue, p. 83

Chalk-hill Blue, p. 84

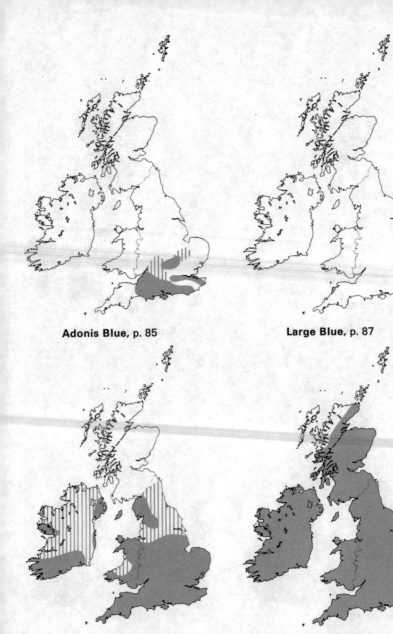

Adonis Blue, p. 85

Large Blue, p. 87

Holly Blue, p. 88

Small Copper, p. 89

Green Hairstreak, p. 91

Brown Hairstreak, p. 92

Purple Hairstreak, p. 93

White-letter Hairstreak, p. 94

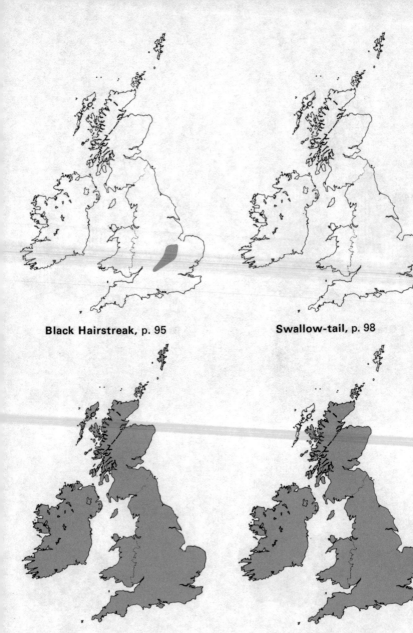

Black Hairstreak, p. 95

Swallow-tail, p. 98

Large White, p. 100

Small White, p. 101

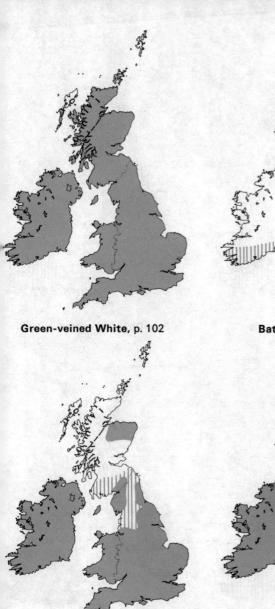

Green-veined White, p. 102

Bath White, p. 103

Orange-tip, p. 104

Wood White, p. 105

141

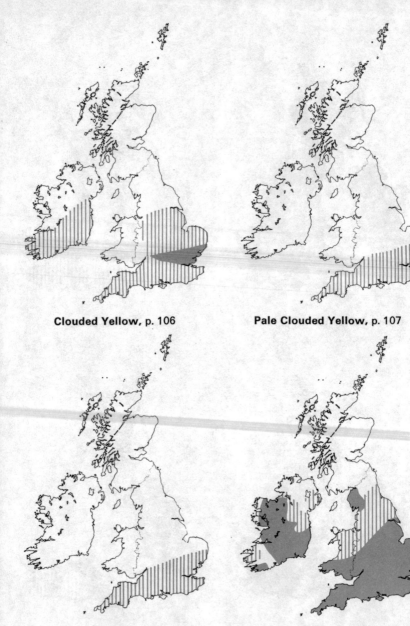

Clouded Yellow, p. 106

Pale Clouded Yellow, p. 107

Berger's Clouded Yellow, p. 108

Brimstone, p. 109

Dingy Skipper, p. 110

Grizzled Skipper, p. 111

Chequered Skipper, p. 114

Essex Skipper, p. 115

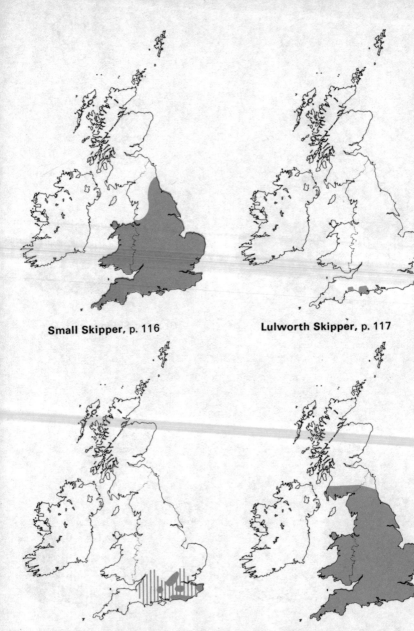

Small Skipper, p. 116

Lulworth Skipper, p. 117

Silver-spotted Skipper, p. 118

Large Skipper, p. 119